I0092840

LOCKDOWN

Journals of Muslim Women
Amidst a Global Pandemic

Edited By
Aishah Alam
Hend Hegazi
F. Akter

Lockdown: Journals of Muslim Women Amidst a Global Pandemic

© 2023 Strange Inc and the individual poets and contributors

All rights reserved. No portion of this book may be reproduced in any form without permission from the individual poet, except as permitted by U.S. copyright law.

Published by Strange Inc, a nonprofit publishing house based in New York. Our mission is to elevate the authentic voices of Muslim women.

Cover Design by BMC Design

Disclaimer: The views and opinions shared in this anthology are those of the authors. Strange Inc does not endorse any personal view of the authors on any platform. Strange Inc adheres to the widely accepted traditional, orthodox doctrine of Ahlus Sunnah.

Table of Contents

Foreword

If we close our eyes and bring ourselves back to March 2020, we might recall a rare and grim realization that settled upon so many of us. In that moment, we knew that we were witnesses to - and participants in - an unprecedented and historic event, one that would be examined, analyzed, and written about in the years and decades following. Across the globe, news media and political leaders presented narratives that were politicized, polarized, and sometimes contradictory. They often ignored or obscured how COVID-19 was experienced on the ground, by real people struggling to keep themselves, their families, and their communities afloat and find meaning amidst danger and despair. What primary sources would future scholars, artists, and citizens turn to in order to understand how the COVID-19 pandemic was experienced on the ground, by everyday people?

Projects like Lockdown , which invited Muslim writers, poets, and performers across the globe to record their lives and their art from March to July 2020, will be an essential text to understand how a group of individuals, tied together by their faith and their creativity, experienced and processed a devastating pandemic. The participants, of 'Lockdown' put pen to paper, fingers to keyboard - or pressed "record" on Zoom or on their Voice Memos app. In doing so, they created the primary sources that show how our pandemic stories are not just about a disease, but about our families and friends, our jobs, our art, our religion, and much more.

One of the most powerful things about this compilation of work is the dialogue we are able to witness between Muslim writers of different cultures and practices, ages and stages of life, and locations and countries of origin. The project demonstrates the remarkable diversity of what it means to be Muslim - but it also reveals a unifying thread of spiritual sustenance and connection with Allah, which is tested but ultimately strengthened amidst the fear and isolation of COVID-19.

Each in their particular voice, the writers of 'Lockdown' looked inward as they looked outward. Spread across the globe, they each experienced a very different Ramadan in lockdown, observing the transformation of tastes, sounds, and rituals amidst the rising COVID numbers. They wrote about the peculiar effects of isolation, the unexpected ways that quarantine transformed their practices and traditions, the stress on family relations and the unexpected closeness the pandemic engendered. They faced death and they welcomed new life. They slowed down, and they created. 'Lockdown: Journals of Muslim Women Amidst a Global

Pandemic' is a beautiful collection of poetry, verse, and reflection. It is also a window into the myriad ways that the COVID-19 pandemic transformed lives, psyches, and artistic practices.

Julie Golia, PhD

Curator of History, Social Sciences, and Government Information at The New York Public Library

chapter one

March 2020

COVID-19 worldwide statistics
for March 2020:[1]

New cases at the start of the month: 2001
New deaths at the start of the month: 64

New cases at the end of month: 74701
New deaths at the end of the month: 3944

1   Source: The New York Times

ENTRY 1

March 5, 2020
Haala Marikar, 19 years old
Sri Lanka

Tell me, child of war,

How do you smile?

You flee

Continents and countries,

Cross the seas

To be called a refugee,

Get tossed into camps,

Stuck in alien lands.

Tell me, child of war,

How do you smile?

You tell me,

"My reward is from my Lord.

Remember those who fled

To Madinah, Abyssinia,[2]

Those who bled

In Badr,[3] Uhud.

My reward as I am displaced,

Distressed, from these wars,

My reward for what I patiently endure,

My reward

---

2   Ethiopia
3   A war during the advent of Islam

Lockdown

Is from my Lord."

Tell me child of war,
How do you smile,
Knowing you were born
After your father passed on,
Leaving your mother to raise you
On her own?
Tell me, child of war,
How do you smile?

You tell me,
"My mother finds strength
In stories of a lady
Who is of the best of all women,
Who was chaste, and conceived,
When no man had touched her,
Who raised her son on her own,
A messenger of the Lord,
Of the best of men.
My mother finds strength
In her story."

Tell me, child of war,
How do you smile,
When your sister is dead,
And your brother is dying,

When you are blind in one eye?
Tell me, child of war,
How do you smile?

You tell me,
"I learnt to smile
From a man who was kind
And compassionate and wise,
Who buried six of his children
During his lifetime,
Who lost both his uncle
And his beloved wife,
Both in the same year.
He had every reason to cry,
Yet, he smiled."

Tell me, child of war,
How do you smile,
When you have so little to smile about,
So little in life?
Your stomach is empty,
You live in a tent,
Your money is spent,
And still, you smile,
So tell me, child of war,
How do you smile?

Lockdown

You tell me,
"My Lord's promise is
That there will be ease
With every hardship,
He tells me,
Don't lose hope, nor despair,
He gives me not a burden I have not the strength to bear.
When His Prophet could still hope
In the belly of a whale,
I know my Lord's promise
Is never one to fail."

Tell me, then, child of war,
When you can endure
So patiently, your lot in life,
When you can smile,
Tell me, child of war,
How can I not?

ENTRY 2

March 5, 2020
Haala Marikar, 19 years old
Sri Lanka

For the past few years now,
Every year,
I've learnt something new.
2018, the word of the year
Was curfew.
Until then I never knew,
In my naivety,
What that entailed.
The stories of 1983,
My parents' accounts of the country aflame,
Was the only reason it was in my vocabulary
At all.
History repeated itself in 2018,
I learnt something new,
The word of the year for me,
Was curfew.

In 2019,
As in the previous year,
I learnt something new.
It was something my country
Was not unfamiliar to,

Lockdown

But had not seen for a decade,
The word of the year, for me,
Was terrorist.
This time curfew
Was a less novel experience.
We installed Telegram[4]
Beforehand,
Since we knew
Social media bans
Were imminent.
In 2020,
As in the years gone by,
I learnt something new.
The word of the year for me
Was quarantine.
Oh, and curfew.
But like I said, past experiences
Take away from the novelty.
Anyway, this year perhaps was the greatest contributor
To my vocabulary.
Quarantine, social distancing, medical terminology.

I hope next year, In Sha Allah,
We'll have a simpler word,

---

4   A messaging app which doesn't permit any outsider to look into some-
    body's visits

A simpler world.
I was thinking
maybe next year can be
"Daisies" or "spring"
Or "baking" or...
Some inconsequential thing.
Because curfew, terrorist, quarantine,
These are big words, I think.
But what I didn't realize
Is that these words did not
For me, at least,
Carry dictionary definitions.
So year of the Curfew meant
More than government regulations,
Year of the Curfew
Was also when we re-amended
Inter-faith relations,
As one faction fought and rioted and burned down homes
and stores,
The others came together,
More than ever before.
Year of the Terrorist,
There were riots, there were deaths,
We all collectively mourned our brothers
Because there's nothing like shared trauma
To bring people back together.
And now, year of the Quarantine,

Lockdown

What are we going to achieve
Is the question.
We find our greatest strengths
When we are tested with tribulation.
You see,
We can have a word of the year
But that doesn't mean
We can't give it our own definitions.

Chapter Two

April 2020

COVID-19 worldwide statistics
for April 2020:[5]

New cases at the start of the month: 77451
New deaths at the start of the month: 5168

New cases at the end of the month: 88522
New deaths at the end of the month: 5946

5   Source: The New York Times

ENTRY 3

April 23, 2020
Maman Kabah, 25 years old
New York

I can't believe that Ramadan[6] is literally a couple of hours away!

I don't know how to feel... I'm not sure whether I am prepped enough for it or not. The only thing I do know for sure, is that it's going to be different — since we are on lockdown.

What I am feeling in my heart is serenity. Serenity that this Ramadan will be filled with ease for some even though it will be a challenge for others, depending on the family dynamic.

I am curious to see what happens this Ramadan.

At 9:00 p.m. today, I wasn't sure how we were going to pray the taraweeh prayers[7] and it was bittersweet; the first prayer for welcoming Ramadan will be at home and some families won't have the opportunity to pray it.

Alhamdullilah[8] my dad led us in prayer.

I was a little surprised because I wasn't sure he was going to do it. I am grateful he did, and I am grateful that someone in the house knows how to do it.

---

6   The holy month where Muslims fast
7   Voluntary prayers offered in Ramadan
8   All praise to God

ENTRY 4

April 24, 2020
Maman Kabah, 25 years old
New York

Ramadan Mubarak![9]

Alhamdullilah for another Ramadan.

I am nervous and overwhelmed because I'm not sure where to start in terms of worship.

There's so much to do, yet being the procrastinator that I am, I tend to hold off on things of importance.

I haven't set up real goals, but I do have some things in mind.

I'm just taking it easy and going day by day. I learnt about what I want to change and what I hope to accomplish even after Ramadan. Ultimately, I just want to be CONSISTENT.

My dad led the taraweeh prayers again, and it was good.

---

9   A greeting Muslims say to each other during Ramadan

ENTRY 5

April 24, 2020
Naimah Baptiste, 32 years old
New Jersey

Which of the favors of your Lord will you deny?

At -Tawwaab?[10] Al-Jawaad?[11] Al-Wahhaab?[12]
Allah tells us in the Quran time after time...
Yet we still deny... deny... deny...

Allah has blessed us with His mercy, Ar- Raheem,[13]
His love, Al-Wadood,[14] His forgiveness, Al-Ghafoor,[15]
Yet, ungrateful are we to our creator, Al-Khallaaq.[16]

Oh children of Adam so easily we forget,
Forgetting our bulging bellies, full freezers, luxurious lives,
packed pantries,
Our children, our homes, our beauty, our youth, our health,
our friends, our family.

Oh Allah! We have earned your wrath,
Locked in quarantine, this is a test!

---

10   One of the 99 names of God, meaning: The Ever Pardoning
11   One of the 99 names of God, meaning: The Magnanimous
12   One of the 99 names of God, meaning: The Supreme Bestower (of gifts)
13   One of the 99 names of God, meaning: The Especially Merciful
14   One of the 99 names of God, meaning: The Most Loving
15   One of the 99 names of God, meaning: The Great Forgiver
16   One of the 99 names of God, meaning: The Creator

Lockdown

Allah has ordained us to stay at home testing us with what
we love the best.

There is a calmness and a slowing of time,
Forcing us to look within to build our eman.[17]

With every hardship there is an ease,
And the blessing of time has now been decreed.

Once a fast paced life stood in all of our paths,
Allah has given us a second chance to reconnect,

There is time to talk, time to read, time to fulfill all your
Islamic needs.
Allah has given us His mercy, Ar-Raheem.
This test can be an opportunity.

In this lesson, we are reminded of His power over everything, Al-Muqeet,[18]
that He is the first and last, Al-Awwal[19] Al Aakhir,[20]
that he is the Granter of Security, Al-Mu'min.[21]

Allah slowed us down for a reason,
the purpose unknown,

---

17   Faith
18   One of the 99 names of God, meaning: The Sustainer
19   One of the 99 names of God, meaning: The First
20   One of the 99 names of God, meaning: The Last
21   One of the 99 names of God, meaning: The Bestower of Security

But reconnecting with our creator, Al-Khallaaq, is needed, an undeniable need.

Which of the favors of your Lord will you deny?

We have sinned, our ungrateful behavior so obvious and bold

Like our denial.

Al-Haadee,[22] please forgive us.
Ameen[23]

---

22   One of the 99 names of God, meaning: The Guider
23   Amen

ENTRY 6

April 24, 2020
Aishah Alam, 31 years old
New York

Yesterday was the first day in over a week—maybe even two—that I went outside for a walk with my one year old.

When I came back, I was exhausted.

I'm not sure if this is because I'm in my third trimester of pregnancy or because I am really out of shape (I'm going to say both).

Saying this, all I can remember from our short walk was how my one year old's little legs (which had just got the hang of walking) were still wobbly in their steps.

She got so excited she would just run... and then fall... and then her determined face would scrunch up as she forced her body to get up. Then she would try to run again, and of course fall.

Ahh baby, always trying to run before you can walk.

I couldn't help but think, isn't that the nature of man? Of woman? The fact we rise, and we fall, and we rise, and we fall until we learn to stand strong, mastering our bodies, our souls.

Seeing my little one, in her moments of learning, I saw so many parallels to our own humanity, our relationship with our own parents and our relationship with God.

Every time she fell, I would instinctively run to her and she would look at me, and I would pretend I wasn't worried.

I know she felt a graze on her little legs, but she copied my reaction and got right back up and toddled along.

Toddled... a perfect word for that walk.

Or should I say waddled?

Yes, waddled. Mummy and baby waddled back home together.

ENTRY 7

April 24, 2020
R Jahan, 38 years old
New York

Pandemic Life, Life with Chronic Illness

I was 9 and in fourth grade when I heard about Magic Johnson being diagnosed with HIV. Back then, it was a death sentence. The news really affected me. Around the same time (or months earlier), my village storyteller died. He had inspired me to write stories telling fables by the pit fire as we roasted potatoes in the courtyard of my paternal grandparents' farm compound at night.

Death was new to me in 1992. So were Pandemics. I had only been to one funeral: that of my great-grandmother, soon after the wedding of her granddaughter, my first-cousin once removed. The AIDs Pandemic was the first Pandemic I had ever heard of. It was scary.

Around the same time, my oldest sister came home with chicken pox she had contracted from a classmate. Despite having a very mild case, I became sicker and sicker. After exposure to more infections and toxins and after 9/11, I had various health problems and autoimmune conditions with a total health breakdown by 2004.

I graduated from a top university with double degrees

and honors but I couldn't work or get out of bed without difficulty. I had to sleep a lot but still felt exhausted. Chronic fatigue and excessive daytime drowsiness made my so-called life a hell for years. Even now, I struggle.

So as the Novel Coronavirus Pandemic began, I realized Pandemic Life and Life with Severe Chronic Illness were a lot alike. Many people are complaining about not being able to go outside or socialize and about having to wear masks. There are protests against mask mandates. People are breaking the stay-in-place order and having large illegal parties. Most people cannot handle Pandemic Life well.

But those of us who live with hard to treat and incurable chronic illness are used to living like that and being partly or completely homebound, and even having difficulty breathing. Not being able to socialize. Not being able to travel or go on vacations. Not being able to shop or have enough groceries or cooked food. Not being able to earn money or get our rightful benefits. Been there. Done that.

Now if we could be done with this new Pandemic! If only I knew the cure to the Pandemic. If only the news would not show trucks waiting for bodies outside local hospitals, as if the whole of New York City has turned into a morgue or funeral home.

Now death is a daily news story and the Pandemic has only just begun. I wish for my old life back, even though it was no fun with chronic illness. The Pandemic has made life for those of us living with chronic illness more difficult. Wearing a mask is uncomfortable but I do it to protect myself and others. Getting groceries is scary but some programs deliver groceries and meals.

I, like so many others, am learning how to survive Life during Pandemic like I learned how to survive "Life" with Chronic Illness. I will not dignify a death-in-life with the term Life. Because feeling and being alive is one of the greatest feelings—one I hardly still experience. So Pandemic Life and Life with Chronic Illness are practically the same to me.

ENTRY 8

April 25, 2020
Maman Kabah, 25 years old
New York

After Fajr,[24] my parents, my aunt and my sister went to a food fest to buy tons of stuff for Ramadan. It was EARLY and I hadn't slept the whole day. We stood in line for 2 whole hours! Can you believe that?

I had to grab dates (I love breaking my fast with dates) and the guy managing the line told us the truck driver passed away not too long ago from COVID 19. Things got really real for me then.

Before going to the food fest, my friend shared a post about a sister we knew that passed away back in October, and it brought back feelings that I didn't want to feel.

I don't know how to deal with death.

Usually I try and forget, even though I think about the deceased every day. I saw a picture of the sister and me with a couple of other sisters from the college we went to. This sister led halaqas[25] and what I remember most about her was her smile, how she smiled all the time. I also remember how passionate she was about the Deen.[26]

---

24   The first prayer of the day; the dawn prayer; also referred to as 'fajr'
25   Get togethers to gain knowledge about Islam
26   Religion of Islam

May Allah forgive her and grant her al Jannah firdous.[27] I'm still learning to deal with death. It is painful.

On a brighter note, I did taraweeh prayers by myself today since my dad isn't home all the time. I was SUPER nervous and scared (but I'm happy I did it).

Today I learned what I need to work on in terms of personality, how I need to be patient and to not stepsons[28] every time someone says something slick. Going to food fest with my family taught me that.

---

27   The highest level in heaven
28   Get annoyed

ENTRY 9

April 25, 2020
Naimah Batiste Mohammed, 32 years old
New Jersey

That morning after suhoor[29] at fajr[30] time, I thought my mama was crazy.

We all thought she was a sleep deprived lunatic!

She had woken up every morning at 3 a.m. to make us breakfast, read the Quran[31] and then go to work.

Our family loved going to the Masjid[32] every night during Ramadan (I thought it was because Papa was cheap and we would eat the free food at the masjid) and well, even though the food did play a large role, the truth is, my parents loved the Quran's[33] message and the sunnah which is the life of the Prophet (peace be upon him).

Prophet Muhammad (peace be upon him)[34] brought people together from every corner of the earth. *I guess we are religious.* I thought to myself.

Mama sniffed the air. She turned in a random direction as if trying to catch a whiff of something but somehow the origin was unclear.

---

29 The meal muslims eat in the morning before dawn before fasting
30 The dawn prayer
31 The holy book of guidance for Muslims
32 The Muslim house of worship
33 The holy book of guidance for Muslims
34 Refers to Muhammad, the last messenger of Islam

"Allahu akbar"[35] was the sound we heard and then Papa began the Fajr prayer and we all followed.

From the side of my eye, I could see my mama's smile and hear her deep inhales as if she were catching a whiff of a delicate delicacy or a rare flower with the aroma of sheer beauty...

"As salaamualaykum wa ramatullah,"[36] Papa's face turned to the right, sending peace.

"As salaamualaykum wa ramatullah," Papa's face turned to the left, sending peace.

"Do you smell that?" Mama's tired eyes sparkled brightly in the dimly lit prayer room. Everyone strained to look at her with their heavy eyelids.

"Do you smell it? I have only smelled that scent once as a child!" she exclaimed in excitement.

She was beginning to get anxious however, hoping that someone else smelt the scent that lingered but was now slowly disappearing.

I shook my head no as kindly as I could.

Hanna's head was in my mama's lap fast asleep.

"I smelt that scent when I was a child, only once before," Mama said again, her teeth sparkling, eyes reflective. "I think an angel prayed with us." Mama smiled cheerfully.

---

35 Allah is the greatest
36 May God put peace and His mercy upon you- this is how Muslims end the prayer

Papa, who doesn't believe in stuff like that, just looked at mama. (He's the kind of man who needs facts; I guess that's where my sister Hanna got it from).

I was intrigued and said, "Really Mama, what did it smell like?"

She smiled and tried her best to explain it. "It's the freshest and cleanest scent you could ever smell. It isn't like anything you have ever smelt in this world. It's almost... like a distant memory. I can't really explain it." She looked puzzled.

She was never at a loss for words, I thought to myself.

"Ok that's enough!" Dad said. "You need to go to sleep, love. You better call out from work."

ENTRY 10

April 25, 2020
Aamila Sameem, 24 years old
Sri Lanka

Where's the vigorous writer in me?

Slugged or dissipated?

Where's the dexterous poet in me?

Dwindled or frazzled?

Have I disorientated to the world of pandemic?

When will I accord the birth of the writer?

Will I ever be enabled to reconnoiter the root as an Ink Slinger?

Where's the convivial[37] self me?

Have I lost it to the diseased world?

Will I ever be able to re-establish the amiability?

Because I've incepted the social distancing from art and buoyancy,

When will I perceive the caress of my passion...

And enliven from the drowsiness of the pandemic war?

---

37   People or occasions that are pleasant, friendly, and relaxed

ENTRY 11

April 19, 2020
Kashmir Maryam, 30 years old
Philadelphia

These days I hear the birds more,
And I hear from people less.
The night chases away the day,
The days chase away the nights.
The two merge so seamlessly
Between the black and white
And gray areas.
Running the course of nature
Yet mankind is most defiant
Against divine order.

ENTRY 12

April 26, 2020
Kashmir Maryam, 30 years old
Philadelphia

To many, a home is freedom. To others it is a prison.

The facemask in some countries is protection. To others, it is seen as oppression. As the saying goes, two men look out from behind bars—one sees the gutter, the other sees stars.

For me, the quarantine has given me some moments alone with my thoughts. But beneath the chatter is an aching soul. I remember that a believer always thinks positive of a predestined decree, but I also cannot help thinking that my Lord is angry with all humanity for the destruction that our lands have committed in the test of comfort. Now we must bear some consequences, before the next world.

Today I sit in concern of what my deeds have brought forth, in fear of the divine retribution. But tomorrow, I will reserve hope.

ENTRY 13

April 26, 2020
Naimah Batiste Mohammed, 32 years old
New Jersey

A nod to my Freedom Riders,[38]
freedom fighters
allowing us Freedom Writers
to express our unique minds.

A nod to the women and men
who fought back then
to preserve my rights, right now.

They were met with violence
to uphold a silence
that boiled and burdened their souls.

A nod to the Freedom Riders,
who were freedom fighters,
who allowed me to unburden my soul.

The Freedom Riders
were freedom fighters

---

38   Civil rights activists who rode interstate buses into segregated southern US cities in 1961 to challenge the non-enforcement of the Supreme Court decision that declared segregated facilities for interstate passengers illegal

Lockdown

allowing Freedom Writers
to express their views.

The views of little Black girls and boys
who had no toys
living in segregated poverty,
who never made the news,
unless to express biased views
to perpetuate hate,
homegrown terrorism meant to discriminate
against those of us who have darker hues.

The Freedom Riders
were freedom fighters
allowing Freedom Writers
to express their views.

The views on immigrants
affecting our nation
from a perspective once untold.

Another version of freedom
because their hue was lighter
than those who fought before,
but still oppressed
and we should cause unrest
to uphold the gift received.

A nod to the Freedom Riders
who were freedom fighters
who allowed me to unburden my soul.

The freedom here
is freedom earned,
not freedom given,
allowing the platform for The Strangers,
our voice.

The Strangers,
us strangers,
possibly Stranger Things
hearing voices behind veiled walls,
opening portals of opinions
of those silenced, wayward, written words
unwrapping American perspectives of:
The Stranger.

A nod to the Freedom writers,
The Stranger writers,
expressing their quarantined views,
allowing all writers
to express the fighter quarantined within them too.

Freedom here
is freedom earned,
not freedom given.

Lockdown

Your silence is a tool of omission,
be the stranger, be the strange.

Inspire your girls and boys,
raise up your voice,
be heard,
because we have sat in silence and whiteness stranger things.

We have witnessed,
false freedom,
graceful genocide,
optimistic oppression,
pretty pandemics,
silent slaughter,
wonderful wars.

Freedom here
is freedom earned,
not freedom given.
Your silence is a tool of omission,
be the stranger, be the strange.

Empower your women and men,
stand up,
be loud,
be seen,
because we have sat in silence and whiteness stranger things.

ENTRY 14

April 27, 2020
Naimah Batiste Mohammed, 32 years old
New Jersey

Never was I the kind to have friends,
Busy was I with life and a husband,

Raising my kids to be on the deen,[39]
Fighting to be on the siratal Mustakeem,[40]

Then...

They came along and changed my mind forever,
Now I make duaa for us to be in Jannah[41] together...

She is kind,
The kind that reads your face: anger, love, anguish, laughter,
She is a keeper,
A keeper of secrets
chapters of you untold,
loving you regardless of what she has been told.

She is real,
Really honest

---

39   Religion
40   The straight path
41   Heaven

tells you the truth when you need it the most,
keeping your nafs[42] from allowing you to boast.

She is a reminder,
She reminds you to recite Quran[43]
and helps you practice,
she corrects your tajweed[44] and is never harsh.

She is extra,
Extra when it comes to her salah
always remembering the Sunnah rakat.[45]

She is encouraging,
Encouraging you to follow the Prophets Sunnah[46]
incorporating his life into our daily works.

She is fast,
Fasting on Mondays and Thursdays,
reminding you the night before.

She is crazy,
Crazily brilliant in everything,
writing, analyzing.
She is bold,

---

42   Soul
43   The book of guidance for Muslims
44   Correct pronunciation of the Quran
45   A single iteration of the movements and supplications performed during the
     obligatory prayer
46   Example

Bold in truth and does what is correct,
and I wonder how someone so brilliant wants to be friends
with me.

She is glowing,
Glowing with Nur,[47]
not from blush or a Fenty stick that many have tried to replicate,
her glow is Allah's gift.

She is reliable,
Reliable and anticipates your needs,
and when you're in a bind she says,
"Don't worry. I got you."

She fights,
Fights you to pay the bill,
her generosity is ongoing and sincere.

They are never hypocrites, or ones to gossip.
They know haters will hate
but hate never won a topic worthy of discussion from their
tongues or lips.
Forever connected and forever bonded by one commonality: Islam ...

---

47   Light of faith

Lockdown

Our belief and way of prosperity.

Oh Allah, keep me in good company and preserve our friendships.

Ameen, Ameen, Ameen.

ENTRY 15

April 28, 2020
R. Jahan, 38 years old
New York

Ramadan[48] in Quarantine might sound like a horror story
or a disappointment
but keep faith in Allah and hope for better
and things will be fine In Sha Allah.[49]
"*Allah hu Arahman, Araheem*"[50]

Ramadan in Quarantine might sound sinister
or like a disaster
But Ramadan in Quarantine
is still Ramadan.

So remember to pray,
worship away...
Like in any previous Ramadan.

Remember:
Ramadan in Quarantine
is still Ramadan.

---

48   The holy month where Muslims fast
49   God willing
50   God is The Most Merciful and Especially Merciful

ENTRY 16

April 28, 2020
R. Jahan, 38 years old
New York

(Being) Lost in Your maze,
Reminds me there are many ways to amaze
(and to be amazed).

You teach me about love and hate.
About Truth and falsehood.
All that is good.
From You comes all good.
Al Barr.[51]
Give me more good.

Today and tomorrow
the deeds that men
and women do
will catch up with them.
Alhamdulillah[52] for the
wonders of Creation.
Astaghfirullah[53] for the sins
and horrors of creations.

---

51   One of the 99 names of God, meaning: The source of all goodness
52   All praise to Allah
53   May God forgive us

Today and tomorrow
The people and
all that is in the world
will pass away.
Leave room for reflection
And for introspection.
Leave room for mourning
And for moving on too.

ENTRY 17

April 28, 2020
Naimah Batiste Mohammed, 32 years old
New Jersey

Dear Reader,

Today started well. I overslept but managed to get my work done remotely on time. I even finished early. Alhamdulillah.[54]

My sister said a few hurtful things, and I wondered if she meant it. The sad thing is, I think she did. In our mature age, it's sad that childhood issues have arisen.

Alhamdulillah, my girlfriend of true friendship, reminded me that the Sahaba[55] had to fight their family during the battle of Badr[56] and that reminder removed my worries. Not to mention, it's Ramadan, and I am in control of myself. I will not allow anyone to steal my peace. Alhamdulillah for the people in my life who remind me of Allah (SWT)[57] and the Sahabas.

To my dismay, later in the evening some of my students contacted me about cyberbullying. I was shocked as to how they got my cell number but happy they reached out for help. Sadly, a student screen recorded all the evil things

---

54   All praise to Allah
55   Companions of the Prophet Muhammed (peace be upon him)
56   One of the battles during the advent of Islam
57   An acronym for Subhana Watala which translates to: glorious and exalted is Allah

being said. My heart hurt for my student. I was sad that my student didn't tell his/her parents and they were unaware. I was sad that my student felt alone. The awful things that were said by other Muslims—during Ramadan! While fasting!—was appalling. Insha Allah,[58] the truth will come out and all will be rectified. I love all my students, but I cannot condone or overlook any kind of bullying or belligerent behavior. I'm glad they understand that with love comes great responsibility, and I actively practice not favoring any one of them.

May Allah guide my students—past, present, and future—to always be on the straight path, show kindness, be good Muslims, and to do well in school. Ameen.

My evening turned into a calm elevation of my Emaan[59] whilst listening to my love recite Quran during the Tarahweeh[60] salah. I knew my love recited well, but my heart felt full of joy, admiration, and awe not only because of that recitation, but out of gratitude that I made the right choice in marrying him all those years ago.

His love for Allah has brightly shown this Ramadan. I suppose it was always there, but I neglected to see it over the years. We prayed in our "going out" abayas/thobes and savored the time together. My heart was no longer heavy for my students but hopeful for their futures. I hugged my kids

---

58   God willing
59   Faith
60   The voluntary evening prayers Muslims offer in the month of Ramadan

Lockdown

a little tighter, a little longer. And, I relished the moment.

Best,

Naimah

ENTRY 18

April 28, 2020
Amirah Ahmed, 16 years old
Virginia

"Social distancing," they said.
6 feet apart,
I didn't realize people would take the "social" so seriously and let our
relationships slowly drift apart.
Loss of motivation seems to be seeping into talking habits too I guess.
I mean,
Maybe you're doing a detox, that's understandable but... your feed is still
full of fresh commentary
you've left every text on read
and maybe it's all in my head
but... the lack of physical contact seems to have our friendship hanging
on by a thread.
Is it me?

This excerpt is about how a lot of people are struggling with their mental health while in isolation without physical access to their support systems. Recently communication with a close friend of mine has become strained, and it is neither of our faults, but it has led to some...weird/confused/ hurt feelings.

ENTRY 19

April 28, 2020
Aamila Sameem, 24 years old
Sri Lanka

The day dawned with viral news on "lockdown," I was bewildered. I asked my mom about this and even she looked startled for a moment.

We began to occupy ourselves as the busiest bees did, buzzing around the house, and then we left for the supermarket.

Lockdown was made a reality for me when I witnessed the shelves were empty—all except for the pens and books.

I contemplated the actions of people and how they left the physical tools of academia, and I shuddered at the thought of the possible future of "e-learning."

What will then happen to the destitute who are left only with tangible academic resources?

Swiftly, I picked up a pen and a book because my passion for books did not allow me to turn without holding it.

And here I am, inking to you in my journal, where the historical moment of lockdown should be carved.

I feel like I'm stepping into history, like when the whole world witnessed World War I and World War II, when Anne Frank hid away in a dark room and inscribed her name in the literary world for her work, "Diary of a

Young Girl."

Here, I feel I can relate to that concept because we too are under a dark world while fighting against a pathogen.

A question drifts in my mind: When will we be able to return under the sun to nourish our souls and embrace mother nature?

The answer is unknown until the world finds a vaccine!

ENTRY 20

April 29, 2020
Nameera Fatima, 16 years old
India

السلام عليكم ورحمة الله وبركاته[61]

Wishing you a very happy Ramadan![62]

As we all know the world is in a tight corner due to the arrival of the Coronavirus, commonly known as COVID-19.

Everyone is in a state of fear and anxiety.

This type of situation is very rare and all around the world, it is getting worse, day by day.

People are dying by the millions. And the truth is, we cannot escape it. This virus poses a great threat of evil in my country.

To control this situation, to stop people from dying, governments have taken the shocking step of locking down all the countries around the world.

Normally, we spend our holidays enjoying outings and we rarely spend them at home. This test needs to be met with great patience.

Most of my time in quarantine went by like a bul-

---

61   Peace, Gods mercy and blessings upon you
62   The holy month where Muslims fast

let train: days were longer in the beginning, but they seem much shorter now. As time progresses, our daily routine, our schedules, and even the very awareness of our calendars have lost their discipline.

Sometimes there's an anxiety of not being able to meet people and the lack of human touch sometimes haunts me. Then there are times when we take a dip into our creativity to fill that void.

It's been a long month since lockdown began. India has managed to flatten the curve and we are adapting. The extroverts have made peace with social distancing.

Sitting in this quarantine, we have been blessed enough not to face hunger. We have enough fat stored in our bodies to survive for weeks without a lavish meal. Alhamdulillah[63] we have shelter to save us from the intense heat of the day.

Of course we cannot forget about the poorly people who need emancipation from this quarantine. It is like they are stuck in the sea and traveling through time. May Allah (SWT)[64] have mercy on them.

Sitting in this quarantine, I have been thinking about what was happening in Kashmir just a few months before the arrival of COVID-19. Ten thousand additional troops from India were deployed there and the schools, colleges, and

---

63   All praise to Allah
64   An acronym for Subhana Watala which translates to: glorious and exalted is Allah

offices were hit hard by them. This led tourists to evacuate and the telephone and internet services were suspended. Regional political leaders were also placed under house arrest.

The people of Kashmir were in lockdown for more than a month, and this was not to save them from any of the calamities, but it was to finish them, to destroy them. The Kashmiris have been in lockdown since August of last year.

I cannot help but think how ironic it is that every politician behind this atrocity regarding the Kashmir conflict is now quarantined in their own homes. Every dog has his day, and it looks very much like this is justice from God; now these very people feel like they are being oppressed by the government, even though this is for their safety.

These last 30 days have been a blur.

I feel sluggish and I know others do too.

I feel like we should thank Allah (SWT) that we are not among those who have been met with this malignant virus. May Allah (SWT) grant health to all those people around the country, Ameen.

As I experience this holy month of Ramadan, I know this is a month of great mercy from God. I pray God brings great happiness to all the people and heals them too. Ameen.

In Sha Allah[65] soon, we will be liberated from this lockdown and we will soon gain control over this virus.

Allah has fashioned the human so perfectly, all of us

---

65   God willing

are perfect and beautiful in our unique way.

This is our fifth day of fasting.

We have been honored with the arrival of Ramadan and this is something to be so grateful about, especially when we consider all those souls who did not get to see it this year.

I pray we can take advantage of this blessed race to His pleasure and utilize our time wisely before another Ramadan comes by. May we be fortunate enough to witness it.

We need to know the destination of this journey of life and where we are headed. I say this because in the situation we are in right now, just as every coin has two sides, there are positives and negatives, and it is easy to forget the ultimate purpose of our existence.

The negative side of this scenario is that most people are suffering and dying from this deadly virus, COVID-19. Happiness has turned to fear and anxiety. However, what about the positive? Ramadan in isolation does just that: cuts us off from the outside world. This can be a good thing as we will no longer be distracted by the things which seem attractive but are not good for us. This is a very big opportunity for us, and we must build a stronger connection with Allah (SWT) and be closer to Him than ever before.

To do this, we need to reset our priorities, and this is through disciplining ourselves.

My advice to all is, be focused on your ibadah.[66]

---

66   Acts of worship to God

Lockdown

These days are the purest blessings.

Remember all the ummah[67] of Muslims in your supplications.

Best regards,

Nameera Fatima

---

67   Nation

ENTRY 21

April 29, 2020
Aishah Alam, 31 years old
New York

I have lost count of how many days we have been in lockdown.

I do however know that of the days, I have experienced six days and seven nights in the month of Ramadan.[68]

It is 10:33 p.m. and as I settle down for the night, I realize that it is raining outside.

Though the world is supposed to be on pause, I can still hear the loud engines of the cars driving by behind my apartment in New York. They drive with an urgency which you would have thought would be homeward bound yet the revving of the motorcycles on any given night and the exhausts of the latest Subaru rave on despite the lockdown. (I cannot say I feel happy about this, I have a one-year-old who is sleeping, and is easily awakened.)

Thinking this, I remember the days I was just like that. I had no care in the world—it was MY world. Childish thoughts for a careless mind. A mind that was filled with so much except a unifying factor. So many thoughts bouncing around with no binding upon them. No real foundation.

Then it all changed.

---

68   The holy month where Muslims fast

Lockdown

By the mercy of Allah, I was shown the truth. Before I continue, I must state that this is not an entry to my journal of victory and end, but rather a beginning and a never-ending battle within myself to not go back to that primal state of mind.

The veil was lifted.

I had been so lost, only He knew how to council me—to guide me.

When the outbreak of this virus first dawned, I remember hearing people say that it was a punishment. They said it was a message from God to people who were doing no good. They said it was an affliction to the people deserving of it, people like those who were trying to rewrite the words of God, people like those who locked up the innocent for no other reason but the choice of their faith.

However, as the virus progressed, it proved that it did not discriminate, infecting the rich of the royal families, prime ministers of various countries, celebrities, and also the poor. It affected the righteous and the sinners. Though in truth, we are all sinners.

So how could this be a punishment? Only punishment?

I then read a Hadith[69] which states that something like this virus can be a punishment or a test. Although we may never know if this is a punishment, I am sure it is a test.

---

69   Sayings of the Prophet Muhammed (peace be upon him)

I was listening to a lecture by Sheikh Hatem al-Haj who himself had the virus, and he said something profound. He said: we will know by the end of this event, where we stand within all of this calamity. Did we use our time wisely? Did we use it not so wisely?

What will I have to show with my time?

As this blessed month of Ramadan has approached us, I feel like the shade of Allah's mercy weighs heavily upon us all.

People message in WhatsApp groups and social media that they hope that Ramadan will bring great blessings to us, but it is not Ramadan, nor an event like this pandemic which brings anything to us. These are all a means; it is Allah who brings His mercy.

I also want to give mind to those who have been through much hardship through this pandemic: many have lost their jobs, many have lost their health, many others, their lives.

I pray Allah brings His mercy to those who have died from this virus and those going through hardship, true blessings from Him. Ameen.

ENTRY 22

April 30, 2020
Aishah Alam, 31 years old
New York

It is 10:13 p.m. and today everything seems to have happened later than usual. Funny how we can be at home but sometimes feel busier than if we were outside. I wonder where the time goes!

Time.

It goes.

As I write this, I am filled with a feeling of urgency: time is leaving! I must take it and use it. I must use it properly, productively and rightfully, whilst giving the rights of all those around me, including myself.

I am exhausted right now, and although this is normal for this late in pregnancy, it doesn't help in making me feel better. I feel useless. I feel like I am wasting so much time resting and every time I try to push myself to do something, I have so little energy.

Saying this however, I have begun to value the gift of will—the will to WANT to do something, and of course the actions in being able to do them.

I have to remember that in these moments, when I feel such heaviness and even the act of standing up becomes a task, it is ok. I just need to do what I am able to.

I also need to remind myself that this feeling is temporary, and in just a few weeks, I'm going to meet her.

Pregnancy is an interesting thing. It makes me acknowledge how perfectly everything is made and prepared for what is meant to be, this new life.

In the beginning, I felt that fatigue, but because at that time, the fact you are carrying a baby is hidden, a secret that no one can see and only you can feel, people underestimate how much it takes from you. They forget that the beginning is the most important part of the pregnancy and this is when the very child is formed from absolutely nothing, clothed with bones and flesh.

Then you have the middle stage where you have this vitality, this energy which pushes you to move forward and get things done. You feel like you can take on the world.

Then comes the final stage, where I am now, and the physical aspect of carrying the extra pounds makes you tired again. With this stage comes a phenomenon called nesting, where you feel the need to prepare; you literally feel like you need to.

Maybe right now, I just need to breathe.

Maybe right now, I just need to trust that Allah[70] will never burden me with more than I can bear. He has never let me down.

Even at times when I didn't get what I wanted, He

---

70   Arabic translation of God

gave me what I needed. And though many have said that before me, I am beginning to have a whole new understanding and appreciation of it.

There are those little things which He does, the ones that if a person did, you would be swept away by their consideration, thoughtfulness and kindness. And all of this is from a Lord whose prayers of ours He does not need, as He showers us—the ones in need of Him—with gifts.

It gives me peace of mind knowing this is my Lord.

We ask and we ask, and He constantly gives.

This leads me to another thought: how praise for us is a dangerous thing.

Someone once said that it is like throwing dust in someone's face because of the harm it causes them. I found it interesting how they said face because that is where the eyes are. It is as if we become literally blinded from the truth of who really is The Most Praiseworthy, by that dirt of praise. That's deep.

So, in those times that I feel fatigued, I hope I can look around and see what I can do to move forward. I hope I can smile as my little toddler waddles to me and points at everything and anything, asking, "What's that?" And as I look closer to what she is pointing at, it is nothing in particular, but rather I realize it is herself: she just wants her mother to carry her and show her the world.

And at the end of a long day like this one, despite all

the goals I tried to achieve and the few that I did, the one thing I think about is that curly haired little girl of mine and how being with her was worth every single minute of my time.

Yes, I can only show her the world for this short time from my windowsill or the occasional walk around the block, but that is our time, and by Allah, this is one of the most beautiful gifts He has given me.

ENTRY 23

April 30, 2020
Aamila Sameem, 24 years old
Sri Lanka

She clicked her camera and began to focus on the Iftar[71] table which was dressed in mouthwatering foods that spread across the table from one end to another with many varieties—some unknown even to her!

She hashtags #IftarSpread and all the other famous iftar hashtags with the strangest of names and she is seen by a *mass* kind of media, where a *mass* number of people like and comment on her post.

Meanwhile, on the other side of the wall, the neighbor wonders what to feed her children for Iftar. Tears flow from her face like a flood from her saddened eyes. Her nose tickles to the aroma of #shorteats[72] and #chickenporridge from next door.

She thinks to herself: Won't the daytime get a little longer? Why is the sunset so early? Is it possible to delay the adhan[73] for Maghreb[74]?

She then shakes her head and realizes it is irrational to give a thought about these things because the times of start-

---

71   The meal that is eaten by Muslims after the sunsets.
72   A type of Sri Lankan street food
73   Call to prayer
74   The prayer at sunset, at which time fasting Muslims can break their fast

ing and ending the fast have been prescribed for us.

The entire day has been gloomy, and now it is Iftar and she breaks her fast with a date and water.

She prepares a small gobbet out of leftover rice and creatively names it Rice-Roti with Chili flakes.

She leaves the children eating at the table and shifts to the Musallah.[75] She raises her hands above her head, and though her stomach grumbles, her heart feels dressed in happiness because she was able to satisfy the hunger of her children.

In the end, the photographed pastries and porridges were thrown into the trash, while the neighbor sighed and blew out her fire lamp, wishing for another Iftar!

---

75   The place of prayer

ENTRY 24

April 30, 2020
Naimah Batiste Mohammed, 32 years old
New Jersey

It is not... the things you see on the TV.

It is not...beds of roses, expensive or grand romantic gestures.

It happens in the unexpected mundane aspects of our everyday life.

It is, thank you and please.

It is, looking at them with respect and admiration.

It is, taking turns washing the dishes because you know they deserve a free moment.

It is, letting them nap and cooking dinner.

It is, listening to them reciting the Quran[76] while pretending not to.

It is, holding hands even though you're sitting next to each other.

It is, looking at each other when speaking.

It is, laughing together and kind words.

It is, supporting their dreams.

It is, overlooking their bad days, truly knowing who they are.

It can be like movies... but that is not our standard.

---

76   The holy book of guidance for Muslims

ENTRY 25

April 30, 2020
Alma Salam, 21-years-old
Sri Lanka

When social distancing became the priority to all, Ramadan[77] did not sound the same to me; the Masjids[78]closed, the Taraweeh[79] were now at home.

Sharing was no longer a good principle. Caring for each other felt like a threat. Streets were empty without noise. Humans searched the net for long-lost relatives and finally found the time to call their long-lost friends.

At this time in quarantine, people were inspired to add great value to human life. An entire globe was forced into lockdown, every single person's future uncertain. And it was then that I began to appreciate the importance of time given to us by Allah.

It is time to flush the sins because no one knows when our time to leave this world will enter upon us.

I used to think that I was too young to think about death but during this time I have reminded myself of the Qur'anic verse which states, "Every soul shall taste death."[80] And it doesn't matter who you are, death can be at any moment. Are we prepared?

---

77   The holy month where Muslims fast
78   Places of worship for Muslims
79   Voluntary prayer during Ramadan is prayed in the evenings, most commonly with others
80   Quran 29:57

Chapter Three

May 2020

COVID-19 worldwide statistics
for May 2020:[81]

New cases at the start of the month: 89018
New deaths at the start of the month: 5277

New cases at the end of the month: 134066
New deaths at the end of the month: 4163

81   Source: The New York Times

ENTRY 26

May 1, 2020
Kashmir Maryam, 30 years old
Philadelphia

Hold me in your prayers

When I am dead and dust

Like bones that come alive

Rising on the tongue of a righteous child

Who prays for the foot under which heaven lies

I am head first in the mud

Clay against clay

The war is only finished when the soul

Is removed from its vessel

Either like a thorn from wool

Or like a droplet of water from goatskin

I am struggling to breathe

Behind masks to protect me from a virus I cannot see

Could

It be racism, Or from Covid-19, 20, 21

That is how young a black man is before he returns to His
creator

Sooner or later anti-blackness is met as a color

Not as cause

You see black people are mothers, humans, believers, lovers, educators, doctors and artists as well as being black.

Before you describe the man or woman who left the room

think beyond the color of their skin
and describe them based on their contribution,
their talent, their poise,
their love, their voice.
There are many things that differentiate between two people.
And I would have failed as a Muslim if I could not reflect
over the political statement of Muhammed SAW,[82] who
told Bilal—a former black Abyssinian slave—to climb the
black ka'bah[83] above the black stone to announce the call to
prayer to a non-black congregation.
And amongst the crowd were murmurs from those of high
bloodlines
astonished, amazed,
silenced, by divine decree
as a black man calls them to prayer.
This is Islam,
It came
To redeem the sinner
To pardon the convict,
To make a martyr of the ego,
To free the supremacist from mental bondage
To enslave the base lower self
So that all that can dance upon this earth
is the sound waves of a sincere servant's tongue and face.
Tongue in cheek as we suppress the irony

---

82   Refers to Muhammed, the last messenger of Islam
83   The holy building in Mecca towards which Muslims across the world face
      to pray. During pilgrimage, Muslims circulate the building.

that slavery was abolished a few hundred years ago, yet still prevails today

In base pay, enslavement to the purchase of commodities to quench consumerism.

That thirst will never end till the mouth tastes between its clenched molars

Dust to dust

From the womb of the earth, to the hearse of the earth.

Will we rise as noble souls, from ignoble births?

ENTRY 27

May 1, 2020
Kashmir Maryam, 30 years old
Philadelphia

COVID:

Never did I think I would live to see

A pilgrim circulating the ka'bah[84] in uniform color-coordinated paths

See when a plague reaches you, it should set about an order
of divine signs

Yet we are so

Quick to think quarantine is for the body

not the soul

Masks all

Colors of the rainbow but

Police brutality color-coded

Programmed to believe inferiority

In darker complexions

But did the night ever compromise its hours

For the sake of a sun whose beams would be too bold for
the white-skinned.

---

84   The holy building in Mecca towards which Muslims across the world face to
pray. During pilgrimage, Muslims circulate the building.

ENTRY 28

May 1, 2020
Kashmir Maryam, 30 years old
Philadelphia

To my Uighur brother, my Kashmiri son, my Palestinian
sister, my Yemeni daughter,

Hold tight onto the rope of Allah.

I know the body that should have protected you is weak,

but we will soon regain our strength.

They say the virus will attack the lungs,

but division attacks all organs in an autoimmune disease of
hypocrisy,

of love for the dunya[85]

and hate for death.

Vast in our numbers,

but like the froth upon the sea.

See we are all sick,

except some diseases are harder to see.

---

85   The worldly life

ENTRY 29

May 1, 2020
Naimah Batiste Mohammed, 32 years old
New Jersey

Dear Listener,

My heart was filled with laughter after Fajr.[86] My daughters shared memories of their favorite teachers' classes and the ups and downs of the school. I laughed until I cried. I wonder if other parents ask their kids how they are feeling and what they missed the most from their "former normal"?

Alhamdulillah,[87] if there was school, my daughters wouldn't have the opportunity to crawl into my bed after Fajr to share stories of teachers, stories of friends and stories of school lunch. They shared the crazy, bizarre, the strange, and the unusual. I laughed with them until my stomach hurt, until tears ran down my face.

There were stories of mischievous behavior, hiding from teachers under desks. Stories of school lunch looking like "clickbait," the picture being the "nailed!" and the food being the "failed it!" They told stories of secret teacher parties for students that ended up not being so secret. There was the last day of school stories, stories, stories, and more stories. I felt happy my girls felt close enough to tell me openly about their bad behavior and mischievous deeds. I

---

86   The dawn prayer
87   All praise to God

listened as a friend, I laughed as a friend, and I conversed as a friend.

Alhamdulillah for all things.

Naimah

ENTRY 30

May 2, 2020
Aamila Sameem, 24 years old
Sri Lanka

I'm thinking of myself as an infant, where I used to be the happiest on earth when I had a carefree life. I am surrounded by blissful faces, clouded with love & affection, and raised with soothing hands. My life is free from all the miseries of the deceitful world, belonging only to the blissed world.

Then my life advances from being an infant to a teenager, and I am deeply moved by my present life as a teenager.

In my life up to here, I see myself as a worried, frenzied, and lost person. I only know heartbreaks and unknown fears such as fear of the world, fear of my existence, fear of fake people, fear of criticism, and fear of pushing away good friends

In the moments of fear, I feel that I've lost myself, I want to regain the power and the faith that I had years ago, before knowing and before meeting the illusionary world!

I see today's world as a complete disaster, molded with delusions, delusions masked in the name of relationships, friendships. I've lost myself to all the ships... I have drowned in the ocean of delusion.

I shove myself vigorously to return back to an unfeigned world that does exist, but only in my thoughts!

ENTRY 31

May 4, 2020
Naimah Batiste Mohammed, 32 years old
New Jersey

Dear Listener,

I'm feeling down today. I spoke with my students and many of them are depressed. I usually coach them through problems at school but I haven't seen them in over six weeks and it's become a real struggle to keep them motivated. They should be making their yearbook and preparing for graduation but now we all feel a little helpless.

Before, they were usually happy for Friday to come and they hated seeing me Monday morning, but now I think they look forward to seeing me online. Some students have come right out and said they miss me and some said they miss my hugs.

I feel helpless. I want to hug them again. I wonder how my students with home problems are doing. Some spoke of the loss of motivation. How can I help when I too have felt that way at some point along this quarantined journey?

May Allah[88] make it easy on them, May Allah make it easy on us all.

Ameen. Ameen. Ameen

---

88   Arabic translation of God

ENTRY 32

May 5, 2020
Naimah Batiste Mohammed, 32 years old
New Jersey

Dear Listener,

Inspiration can be found in the strangest place. After an evening and early morning of feeling defeated, I was looking at pictures of teaching Kindergarten and I realized that I can't let my students down.

They are sad and depressed, and this is why I will continue to strive for ways to make them happy. They need something to remotivate them. This is perhaps one of the most difficult things they have ever faced! Yes, it is going to be a challenge but God willing, they will overcome their negative feelings and I will help. How can I be creative enough to inspire them to do their work and attend a live class? Hmmm, I will make it more interactive, maybe mail things to them? Maybe we can do dress-up days?

Allah is testing our faith, mental strength, and emotional abilities and we WILL get through this!

I will motivate them—God willing.

ENTRY 33

May 5, 2020
Alma Salam, 21-years-old
Sri Lanka

Day by day,

In every person's life,

There was a delay,

All looking for a way,

Because no one is getting any pay,

...One last time

Wouldn't we crave

For back in the old days,

Where social distance didn't matter.

Happiness was scattered

I hope today will get better

...One last time

Just one last time

A time when I was free,

I didn't have anything to see,

Alone it was me

My love for You increased

...day by day

But back in the day,

When I was in my daily chaos

I didn't have time for You

I forgot to praise You

Lockdown

And now when I go deeper and deeper
I realize that Your love for me was greater
Alhamdullilah[89] it wasn't later,
I wonder how...
How could you love and give your mercy to us so much?
I speak of none other than my Rab.[90]

---

89   All praise to God
90   Lord

ENTRY 34

May 5, 2020
Aamila Sameem, 24 years old
Sri Lanka

Reflect on yourself through the verses of the Quran.[91]

That's bestowed down from heaven.

Reflect on your Deen[92] Al-Islam[93]

to revive your character with a slam.

The time you used to make an excuse is no more.

Because you're in self...quarantine.

Yet, self... quarantine

Could be metamorphosed into Quran Time.

Reflect upon you!

Revive your soul without adieu!

You're bestowed with unimaginable time for seclusion

to redirect your path from the traps of Satan.

Contemplate your hearts with the words of Allah[94]

to acquire a position to be under Allah's shade in the Aakhira.[95]

Reflect upon you!

Revive your soul without adieu!

When you're summoned

---

91   The holy book of guidance for Muslims
92   Religion
93   Of Islam
94   Arabic translation of God
95   Afterlife

Lockdown

Time waits for none.
Explore the light of Allah, *Noorullah*[96]
Expedite the words of Allah, *Kalamullah*[97]

---

96   Light of Allah
97   Words of Allah

ENTRY 35

May 5, 2020
Aishah Alam, 31 years old
New York

I am conflicted as to how to write—Yes, HOW to write. Do I write in a way which is beautiful or in a way which is meaningful?

I know it's best to do both but many times it is easy to lose the self in the sentence and when I read it back, there is little that has truly been said.

When I read something that is written powerfully and beautifully, I cannot help but feel admiration for the writer, for the message.

I suppose the best writers to me are those who can say much using only a few words, like the Islamic scholar, Ibnul Qayumm:

> *"This worldly life is like a shadow. If you try to catch it, you will never be able to do so. If you turn your back towards it, it has no choice but to follow you."*

Allah Himself does this in the Quran, a timeless book, one which each sentence can have pages and pages of inter-pretation because of the depth of the speech of Allah.

I will leave it at that for now.

ENTRY 36

May 5, 2020
Aishah Alam, 31 years old
New York

As time progresses, I cannot help but feel an urgency to get all I need to get done.

I am almost 39 weeks pregnant and I feel like a beached whale!

Time feels like it is escaping me. I try to take it, but the hours slip by in the progression of each day.

As time goes on, and even though I feel apprehensive, my breath is short, I am tired—exhausted—with nights filled with insomnia, the need to do something, the feeling like I am doing nothing, but despite all this, I cannot deny the gifts Allah has been giving me.

Through all of this pandemic, the one name of His which I cannot stop thinking about is: Ar Rahim.[98]

My Merciful One.

He has been giving openly and I have been taking with no reservation.

It is so easy to forget the good and focus on the bad, especially when you are surrounded by those who see the world through a critical eye. Some of these blessings are the feelings we have. The peace, joy and hope. We cannot

---

98   The especially merciful.

change the way we have been taught to think—not at first. But we can begin to decide which thoughts control us and which we will not allow to control us. The people we choose to surround us, are in many ways our guides, to either good or bad, and we too play this role for them.

That is why I am seeing more and more how important good companionship is to better ourselves.

That is all from me tonight.

Goodnight.

ENTRY 37

May 6, 2020
Naimah Batiste Mohammed, 32 years old
New Jersey

Icy rage envelopes my body.

My anger heightened, all of my senses on edge and I am fuming!

Why did I press play? I never can bring myself to watch the brutality in others. I always scroll past.

I am furious, seething.

How is it that in 2020, young Black men can't take a jog down the street.

Some might ask why am I so pro-Black? Why am I always talking about race? The reason is simple: because it never stops!

They call this the best country in the world, people around the world desperate to live the "American Dream," "Home of the Brave," "Land of the Free" ... except we are still slaves. Ahmaud Arbery I am sorry you died like that.

He could have been one of my own brothers, who share the same complexion as him and live close to where he was killed.

This realization sends chills so deeply within me, they smash my soul.

The ignorant are threatened by a mere complexion,

what change has really happened after the civil rights? When will we cease the petty racism which causes great atrocities in cruel killings of the innocent?

I need the strength to stand up and RISE!

Bob Marley once said: *"Get up, Stand up, Stand up for your rights, Get up, Stand up, Don't give up the fight."*

It's become so bad that I have to pick up the phone and call my younger brothers and tell them to stay inside. I have to tell them not to go for a simple walk. A walk has become fatal.

And then there are those who throw around the "N" word, I can't believe it! People are still dying for it.

A Citizen Arrested was the front page of a story; the next thing they will say the victim whistled at a white woman.

Billie Holiday sang a poem called "Strange Fruit."

Here is my version in 2020:

The Nations streets filled up high,

Not Roadkill but where black bodies lie,

Strange Fruit, Strange Fruit,

Your color controls your life

Strange Fruit, Strange Fruit,

It's where black bodies lie,

Bloodstained shirts with bullet holes,

They break us down to know our roles,

Mothers scream, their life unfolds.

Strange Fruit, Strange Fruit,

Lockdown

Men hunted down for their dead flesh.
More valuable when lifeless.
No mourning, not depressed
But a prize some hold to their chest!
Strange Fruit, Strange Fruit.
Not much has changed.
Strange Fruit, Strange Fruit.
They beat black bodies every day
Strange Fruit, Strange Fruit,
I bow down my head and pray.
Naimah Baptiste, 2020

ENTRY 38

May 7, 2020
Aishah Alam, 31 years old
New York

Today I found a hole in a book of mine placed near the bottom of the bookshelf. As I examined it, I noticed it was the size of... someone's teeth.

My little girl's teeth.

She had bitten the book cover and with the remnants in her mouth she opened her mouth and ran to me showing me the evidence of her naughtiness.

I wondered why she did this.

I then realized she had noticed how happy I got when she took out inedible things from her mouth, the point being that she shouldn't have been eating it in the first place. But being only one year old, she couldn't make the connection and instead tried to get the positive reaction from the very act which we were trying to stop.

I smiled as I thought of this. I'm smiling now.

How precious and endearing the child is... how innocent.

ENTRY 39

May 7, 2020
Naimah Batiste Mohammed, 32 years old
New Jersey

You want to be down... where are you now?

You want to say the N-word, but would you take a bullet for it?

Didn't think so...

You want to be down... where are you now?

You silently slip back and morphed into something that's easy.

Black bodies, Black bodies piled so high,

It depends on how they choose to kill you, but our bodies die.

Some shot down with bullet holes

Bleeding out their bodies cold.

Some beaten to a pulp at a traffic stop

Officer, you never said you were a cop.

Black bodies, Black bodies,

Some dissected her for her lips

Cut that off, we want her hips

Some tan their skin, just enough

But when times get hard, they rub it off.

Some are shut down, just play your game

N-word, N-word you got no Brain.

Just keep on playing so they are entertained.

Ladies, Ladies, don't be smart,

Take off your clothes, just shake your parts,

Taken without a choice,

Our missing organs and you rejoice,

Institutionalized racism and separated blocks

Similar to those who throw rocks.

Your own leader encourages brutality

The bombs raining down is a reality,[99]

You want to be down... where are you now?

You want to say the N-word, but would you take a bullet for it?

Didn't think so...

---

99   Being bombed is a references to Osage Ave being bombed on May 13th 1985 in P.A

ENTRY 40

May 7, 2020
Aamila Sameem, 24 years old
Sri Lanka

Children of the earth, are you deluged by the war of the virus?

Children of the earth, are you sleeping like the People of the Cave?

Have you forgotten the oppressed in this holy month?

Have you realized what else is happening besides the outbreak?

Do you remember the Uyghur Muslims, Syrians, Palestinians, Rohingya?

What about the Kashmiri & Indian Muslims?

Do you think about them while you're practicing social distancing?

Or

Do you practice social distancing from the injustices around the world too?

Do you anticipate this Ramadan is an unimaginable trial for you without:

Iftar[100] gatherings,

Taraweeh[101] at masjid,[102]

---

100   The meal Muslims eat after breaking their fast
101   The voluntary prayers at the mosque
102   Muslim house of worship

Eid[103] prayer & Eid dress.

Then contemplate about the Uyghur Muslims, Palestinians, Syrians, Kashmiris,

Rohingya who are denied of their basic rights to live as fellow Muslims.

Who are they? What are they doing? Why are they suffering?

Did you ever think that they are under the reign of tyrants?

Haven't you seen what's happening in China?

Uyghur Muslims are denied their rights to practice the religion.

Children are left orphaned,

Women are raped,

Uyghur identity is erased.

Where's the justice?

Where's the freedom?

Is it the resurgence of Islamophobia?

Lobby the world!

Speak for justice!

Do you remember the Palestinians under apartheid for more than half a century?

Do you think they are content beside the Covid-19 pandemic?

Yet, they still continue to suffer not from the outbreak but due to tyranny.

Where's the justice?

---

103   The festive celebration at the end of Ramadan

Lockdown

Where's the freedom?
Is it the resurgence of Islamophobia?
Lobby the world!
Speak for justice!
Haven't you seen what's happening in Myanmar?
Rohingya Muslims are under brutal genocide.
And obliterated from their native land.
Is it a trend of the modern world?
Where's the justice?
Where's the freedom?
Is it the resurgence of Islamophobia?
Lobby the world!
Speak for justice!
Do you remember Syrians who are under a decade-long
civil war?
And still continue to be despite the pandemic.
Have you thought this as a stain on humanity?
Yet, the world considers fantasy rather than the reality.
Where's the justice?
Where's the freedom?
Is it the resurgence of Islamophobia?
Lobby the world!
Speak for justice!
Haven't you seen what's happening in India?
Or
Do you remember Kashmiris who were under lockdown
before you experienced it?

While you're being provided with all the necessities for a modern man,

Kashmiris are denied their basic rights as human beings.

Where's the justice?

Where's the freedom?

Is it the resurgence of Islamophobia?

Lobby the world!

Speak for justice!

Do you anticipate the trial you're in as a tremendous one?

While your brethren around the world continue to suffer under the unending

oppression and injustices?

Don't you see you're in the comfort zone in the blessed month?

Speak for justice!

Seek the Almighty's help!

Stand up for human rights!

Pray for the justice of Allah to surpass the injustices and oppressors.

Pray for the justice of Allah to reign over the Muslim Ummah![104]

---

104   Nation

ENTRY 41

May 9, 2020
Aishah Alam, 31 years old
New York

I keep thinking about two things: patience and gratitude.

I recently read Surah Yusuf[105] and how his father Yaqub[106] spoke of a beautiful kind of patience.

A beautiful patience. What would make it beautiful?

I know that you can be patient in expecting for the bad to happen, but you can be patient in hoping for good too, in believing Allah[107] has an ultimate plan.

Last night my little one was in and out of sleep because she got her vaccines the day before. I think she was in pain but being just a little one, she could not communicate her pains to me.

Only through her cries and then occasional excitement as she laughs gleefully pointing at everything. It is interesting how quickly children can forget their pain in their grip of what makes them curious and happy. In this way, I think we can learn a lot from them.

On the outlook, being a parent is like a hardship.

---

105   Chapter 12 in the Holy Quran
106   Jacob
107   Arabic translation of God

Here we are, being kept from sleep, constantly worrying if our children are ok, trying to give them what is good for them when sometimes we don't even know what is good for us. The hardest thing is being patient with them.

It is being patient with them as a parent and doing it beautifully.

As I write this, I think again of Yaqub and how his most beloved son was taken, and even worse how he knew— he KNEW!—that his other sons were responsible for it. He knew they lied to him. He knew they did not want good for their brother.

And he just turned his face away from them and turned to Allah and said he would have beautiful patience because He also knew that Allah had the best of plans for him.

He knew that Allah would only give him good.

If we as parents can master patience with our children, then I truly believe we can learn to do it in other parts of our lives.

There is a reason why the Hadith[108] of our Messenger[109] regarding how he was best to his wives is so powerful: because it is those close to you who see you for who you truly are, and if you are good and patient with them, then that is who you are.

---

108   A narration of our messenger
109   Refers to Muhammad, the last messenger of Islam

ENTRY 42

May 9, 2020
Amirah Ahmed, 16 years old
Virginia

How can I look on the bright side
when I don't even know if I'll make it to the other side of
this?
It seems like there's no end in sight
And I think I might just be losing my mind
so please forgive me
If my soul doesn't seem just right
If my charisma is a bit off tone
and at this point I've stopped answering the phone
because I can't bear to hear the wondering questions anymore:
"What's going to happen next?"
"Where do we go from here?"

It's a different kind of pain to see your future
your goals
your wildest dreams
crushed under the foot of something
you can't control

I'm a little crushed right now,
so please forgive me

if I'm not at my best
I promise I'll be back
Once my future isn't a question mark...
and my heart can finally rest

ENTRY 43

May 5, 2020
Maman Kabah, 25 years old
New York

This week was interesting and boring to say the least. I'm learning more and more of what I need to improve and trying to break out of bad habits. It's harder than I thought. I can't believe Ramadan is almost over! It feels like it just came. Subhanallah.[110] Most of what I've been doing is sleeping and shopping for food. The days seem shorter and fasting just seems a lot easier. It's probably because we are in quarantine. Almost everyone has a messed-up sleep schedule, and I'm trying to learn how to deal with my own.

---

110   Allah is the most perfect

ENTRY 44

May 9, 2020
Maman Kabah, 25 years old
New York

Oddly today was kind of an adventure. I went to go get some groceries and halal[111] meat in Brooklyn early in the morning. Mind you, I didn't sleep the day before. My good friend drove us all the way to Brooklyn and it was a good journey. I got some fresh air and peace of mind being outside. I went home and went right back out to go buy something to break my fast with. I went with another friend all the way to Harlem. (One thing I won't miss when the quarantine days are over is the lines!) I keep forgetting how long the lines are for food!

---

111   Meat which is slaughtered according to the Islamic way

ENTRY 45

May 10, 2020
Aishah Alam, 31 years old
New York

I'm in labor.

Here it goes.

Bismillah.[112]

---

112 In the name of God

ENTRY 46

May 11, 2020
Aishah Alam, 31 years old
New York

My baby was born at 2:45 a.m. In Ramadan.[113] At the time of tahajjud.[114]

On the same day of the week our messenger Muhammed (peace be upon him)[115] was born, a Monday.

How merciful Allah[116] is. How merciful He is as He answered my prayers with such kindness.

In a matter of hours, labor progressed and before I knew it, there I was, holding her.

My baby girl.

Sister of Barakah.

Descendent of Kashmir and Palestine. (May Allah free them both, ameen.)

As soon as she heard my voice, she turned her head towards me like she already knew who I was. She stopped crying.

When they took her away to weigh her and warm her, she cried again but when the heat went on, she quieted

---

113 The holy month where Muslims fast
114 A part of the night before dawn which is considered sacred because God comes to the lowest heaven to listen to the prayers of his slaves
115 Refers to Muhammad, the last messenger of Islam
116 Arabic translation of God

again, enjoying the warmth. I guess she lives in warmth. I guess she loves love.

My husband gave her a little bit of a date (a sunnah of our messenger) and read the call to prayer in her ear.

The first thing I noticed was her peacefulness.

Her name is Salamah, inspired by Umm Salamah. A woman whose story I heard in increments—I'm a little too exhausted to talk about it right now, but I will. One thing I can share about her now is how I was always in awe of her wisdom.

How she asked if the verses in the Quran[117] referred to women too, and Allah answered her by revealing a verse speaking of the status of both women and men in righteousness. We are equal.

How when her husband died, she couldn't think of being with anyone else because he was so beautiful to her, and then Allah gave her the best of men, our messenger (peace be upon him).

What a woman.

And now, I, mother of Salamah, a word which means peace and tenderness, I am umm Salamah and my husband is Abu Salamah. I pray Allah makes us even half the people they were. Ameen.

117　The holy book of guidance for Muslims

ENTRY 47

May 7, 2020
Aamila Sameem, 24 years old
Sri Lanka

Some people curse me for breaking into their amused lives.
Some grip me tight,

For entering into their glorified lives.

There begins the difference.

Some execrate me, while some consider me a blessing.

Optimistic ones hold me,

to uplift their Eeman[118] from who they are to who they will become on the day of resurrection.

The ones who take me for granted will eventually realize their trespasses on the day judgement.

I'm disguised as a virus to purify your Eeman.

Don't let the days of seclusion

distract you from Allah to Satan.

Don't let yourself get carried away towards the mini theatre

Where you'll find the illusionary movies

While the reality stays behind the curtain.

You, the one who transforms your homes as graveyards.

Have you prepared yourself to meet the Creator?

While you're empty handed.

---

118   Faith

Lockdown

Because the more you indulge in worldly delusions
The more you stray from good deeds.
Act vigilantly! Your day might be tomorrow!

ENTRY 48

May 12, 2020
Amirah Ahmed, 16 years old
Virginia

He is in the worn threads of my mother's work scrubs after
another day of watching the world disintegrate
before her feet.

He is in between the furrowed brows of my father
navigating a sea of uncertainty.

He is in the boisterous giggles that escape my little sisters'
room,
laced with the blissful ignorance of childhood.

He is in the oil that soaks my hair and the face mask seeping
into my skin,
an effort to keep sanity in this insane scenario.

He is in the tears that fall to the prayer mat from my best
friend's eyes,
pleading with Allah to end the rampant fear.

He is the Almighty, the Most Merciful,
woven into the fabric of our lives,

Lockdown

of our hopes,
dreams and despairs.

He is the Giver of Gifts,
so we turn to *Him*,
beg *Him* to bless us with a remedy to our woes
for *He*,
oh *He*, is the Restorer,
the Provider,
the Most Compassionate.

If *He* can craft the
cells that make up
the intricacies of your being...
My dear, won't you have faith
in *His* ability to cure
this predicament we are in?

You must remember during the faithless nights that "Your
Lord has not abandoned you, nor does *He* despise you."
When you cannot find God
look no further
than your jugular vein.

Examine the tips of your fingers
and the curve of your nose,
and tell me then
if you've found the faith

in Al-Musawwir,
the Shaper, the Fashioner.

So find *Him* in the folds of your thobe
and the marble beads with which you
repeat your remembrance.

Find *Him* in the lonely moments
when you think you just can't take
this isolation anymore.

When there seems to be no end in sight,
recall the names of your Lord
Al-Awwal, Al-Aakhir
He is The First and *He* is The Last.

Put your trust in Al-Hakim,
the All-Wise,
for *He* will not fail you
even in the most trying of times.

ENTRY 49

May 13, 2020
Aishah Alam, 31 years old
New York

I have had a chance to breathe! I wrote this post on Facebook announcing my little girl's entrance to the world:

In the midst of chaos, there is a calm in which nature has become predictable in being.

In the tornado is the eye which sits still.

In war there is the peace one envisions at the end of it.

In the storm there is the rain which is nurturing the ground which harvests seeds.

On May 11th, at the time of tahajjud... 2.45 a.m., on a Monday... not Mother's Day but the day of the birth of our prophet peace be upon him, in Ramadan, our baby girl , sister of Barakah and daughter of Kashmir and Palestine... Salamah was born.

In the midst of chaos in this invisible war of a virus.

Where the lungs have been attacked, breaths taken away, the frail made sick, the people of the world upon their knees and this is when Allah brought forth my second child.

My baby girl, Salamah.

Salamah means peace and tenderness.

Salamah, inspired by Umm Salamah who was an icon of Islam.

I am now Umm Salamah, wife of Abu Salamah, praying that we can be half the beacons of Islam that they both were. This was not a name chosen by my husband and I, but by Allah and there is no power nor might except by Allah.

ENTRY 50

May 13, 2020
Naimah Baptiste, 32 years old
New Jersey

I raise my hand up high in humility and cry: "Ya[119] Allah please give them justice, please give them peace. Ya Allah please make it easy on them."
Ameen.
My pain is only a thought. Nothing in comparison for those in Kabul, who survived the massacre in a birthing unit this week.

I wonder, who are you? You savage beast!
The mothers murdered in their beds after they moaned in pain... agonizing pain to give birth.
A schism in her pelvis,
Muscles seized, insides twisting,
Pain to push,
Pushing in pain,
Pulling on her organs as she painfully bears out a tiny person.
Tears of joy upon meeting the person who lived inside her.
Who are you? You savage beast!
Paralyzed with fear,

---

119   Oh

Pleading for her life.

Pleading for her child's life.

To no avail ammunitions released,

Metal projectiles discarded from the cartridge

With no concerns for the soft flesh

Murdered in her bed as she tried to rest.

She will not be discharged with her bundle of joy.

But shrouded in white and met with Janaza salah.[120]

May Allah elevate their status and grant them all the pleasures of the akhirah. Ameen.

Who are you? You savage beast!

New with life, New of life.

Newborn babies you murdered.

Murdered before they learned to open their eyes.

Murdered before learning hunger.

Murdered before learning the sweetness of their mother's milk.

You stole dreams,

You stole hopes,

You stole happiness.

You stole smiles,

You stole safety,

You stole security.

---

120   Funeral prayer

Lockdown

You stole first times,
You stole holidays,
You stole graduations,
You stole weddings,
You stole forgiveness.

Alhamdulillah,[121] and Allah knows best...
Who are you? You savage beast!
In the holy month of Ramadan, you wreak havoc on the most vulnerable and defenseless.
You are an abscess of life,
An infection putrefied sore, oozing a disease of violence and hatred.
You are a hostile evil that creeps into our souls, slithering on smooth surfaces spying for ways to seep into our hearts and souls.
You spit your wicked, vicious, venom, to divert our attention from the truth.
La ilaha illallah, MuhammadarRasulullah.[122]
But we know who you are, from the time you disobeyed Allah and vowed to misguide the children of Adam...
You are a Monster.

---

121   All praise is to Allah
122   There is no God in truth except Allah and Muhammed is His messenger

ENTRY 51

May 15, 2020
Alma Salaam, 21 years old
Sri Lanka

If you make a mistake, my girl,

How do people portray you? Do they make themselves as a legend?

If you speak for your rights,

And if you are controversial,

Do people say that you are not a girl of your deen?[123]

Why do you fear my girl?

Does society point you as characterless when you are exposing wrongs?

Why does today's world victimize the Muslim women?

Doesn't Islam teach not to work for pleasing people?

Didn't people read the pages of history, where Aisha (May Allah be pleased with her)[124] led a war and was a great scholar?

Where Khawla Bint Azwar was a great warrior of Islam?

Where the Qur'an[125] speaks favorably of the Queen of Sheba (Biliqis)?

---

123   Religion

124   Prophet Muhammad's wife and considered as a Mother of the Believers

125   The holy book of guidance for Muslims

Lockdown

Where Prophet Mohammed (peace be upon him) was upset and angry with the sahabhas[126] for not informing him of the death of the woman who cleaned the Prophet's mosque?

Where the first martyr of Islam was Sumaiyah (May Allah be pleased with her)?

Where Nusaybah Bint Ka'ab was the first woman warrior of Islam?

Be the person who Amplifies the voice of women!

Start viewing everything without bias.

Cease misrepresenting women.

It begins with perception. Your perception of life. As long as you have an angle and capture the truth, nothing is impossible, you can change your view of life.

Stand for the truth!

Search for the Deen!

Don't let only what you speak define you!

Let your actions show who you are!

---

126   The companions

ENTRY 52

May 14, 2020
Haala Marikar, 19 years old
Sri Lanka

*"Do they not travel through the earth, and see what was
the end of those before them?"*

-Surah Rum[127]

Today, I reflect

Upon death,

Upon the temporary transience

Of this life,

Here today, gone tomorrow.

Great palaces, and pyramids

And homes, all eroded

With the sands of time,

Ruined, destroyed,

And how many kings and emperors,

Like Qarun[128]

And Fira'un?[129]

How many

Wealthy men, empires, armies,

Must this earth have housed,

---

127   The Holy Quran, chapter 30 verse 9
128   Major figure known for the misuse of his wealth
129   An antagonist in the story of Moses. Also known as Pharaoh.

Lockdown

And in life, they thought,
There was permanence,
And they walked with arrogance?
What is their state in their graves?
Those who were unjust,
To their people and themselves,
What is their state in their graves?
Their fate in their tombs
Of gold and silver and treasures?
But know
Not all the pleasures
Of this world
Will do you any good
If all you have earned is evil.

ENTRY 53

May 15, 2020
Naimah Baptiste, 32 years old
New Jersey

Patience please,

She patiently pleads

Practicing patience purposefully,

She persistently pleads for patience.

Patience please.

ENTRY 54

May 17, 2020
Aishah Alam, 31 years old
New York

What they don't tell you about after pregnancy:

So many things.

I did it once before but for some reason this time things seemed so much different.

I noticed it at the first prick of a needle when getting the routine blood work in the first trimester.

The prick was sharper. I flinched and my skin was bruised for a few days.

When I washed the dishes, I no longer wanted to wear gloves, I wanted to wash them with my hands, mix the batter of the banana bread with my hands, marinate the chicken with my hands. (I did this with my hands anyway but there was a new feel to it.)

When in labor, though the actual labor was, by Allah, an ease in many ways, the effect of the pain medication felt much more potent.

I felt its effects for days after.

This sensitivity was something new to me compared to my first baby.

It is as if all things external to the natural process of my body were painful. My body wanted all that is natural.

You realize through this experience how you truly have no control at all and when you see that child's face, how beautiful it is and how perfectly formed each part of their bodies are—their little toes, their tiny fingers, the way their hair is up to the nape and their little neck folds over in fat, the cheeks you will kiss and the eyes which are round and huge looking up at you in familiarity as you look and see your own eyes within them—this you know is not from ourselves. It is from none other than Allah.

It *could* be from none other than Allah.

From nothing and now this, which grows to be us: me and you.

With my first precious blessing, I was impacted with the emotional part of it all. The pain was tolerable and dare I say even empowering.

For this baby, the pain was tolerable too but more memorable. Reminder: Allah does not burden one with more than they can bear.

I wonder if my reactions to the things around me were influenced by the qualities they will carry in life: the cravings, the pain tolerance and the crazy emotions.

My first has a high pain tolerance and is a strong one, Allah humma barek,[130] but this one seems more vulnerable,

---

130   May Allah bless [her]

even her cries pang my heart to want to run and take care of her because she needs me.

The plights of a mother I suppose.

And on that thought, what about the names we give our children? It's interesting how we grow up being so focused on who we are and our identity and at times even rude and cruel to those that bore us. I'm guilty too.

But with every call a person refers to us as, with every identification badge, comes the question, who are we? We are our parents' children.

We are even named by them carrying their marks upon us, no matter how much we try to escape.

I believe this is a sign.

A sign of how important it is to know ourselves—our names and our heritage.

May Allah bless our mothers and our fathers, ameen.

And as I once said to a fellow freedom writer, we will never stop being our parents' children.

Would I do it all again if it meant my baby was healthy?

In the blink of an eye.

ENTRY 55

May 17, 2020
Naimah Baptiste, 32 years old
New Jersey

My enjoyment is of thou's fondness,

Tenderly appreciating my devotion as a delight,

Doting on my warmth,

Relishing in my tenderness,

Smitten by adoration,

In awe of your affection.

ENTRY 56

May 18, 2020
Naimah Baptiste, 32 years old
New Jersey

Scrubbing, rinsing, washing.

Is your heart as immaculate as your floors?

Salah,[131] Siam,[132] Zakat.[133]

Are they said daily, done on time, paid in full?

Have you disinfected, sterilized and decontaminated your soul?

Sweeping, dusting, polishing.

Thikr, Istiadhah, Adhkar.[134]

---

131 Prayer
132 Fasting
133 Charity
134 Way of praising and remembering Allah

ENTRY 57

May 18, 2020
R. Jahan, 38 years old
New York

Allah Tells us to fast in Surah Baqarah[135]
so that we may attain taqwa.[136]
Fasting is more than refraining from food.
It is also about doing more good.
As we deny our bodies food and water,
we make our souls stronger and better.
Allah made the month of Ramadan
The Month of The Quran.
Allah Made the Quran, the Furqan.[137]
It is the criterion between right and wrong
So we can strive for Jannah all along.

---

135 Chapter two in the Holy Quran
136 God consciousness
137 The criterion, proof, evidence, testament

ENTRY 58

May 19, 2020
R. Jahan, 38 years old
New York

Allah Creates.

People imitate.

Allah Creates mates.

People create divorces.

Allah Gives peace.

People create chaos.

Such imperfect creations

From a Perfect Creator.

Seems so unfair, so ungrateful,

So better yourself now before later.

ENTRY 59

May 19, 2020
Amirah Ahmed, 16 years old
Virginia

Passive aggressiveness.

Inferior correctness.

Pent up expressiveness.

Your emotions are in quarantine,

so we face the brunt of your hotheaded manhunt,

your search to find any innocent

and make them feel your misery,

stamp on their soul,

trample across their last shreds of sanity.

In your mental warfare nobody can be happy

unless you are

but you're as miserable as can be

so here we are left searching for serenity

in the safe space of salah

and hours during which you slumber.

Recharge with as much patience as possible

cause soon as sun rise,

we must face no man's land

walking on eggshells

careful to not set off the grenade

ENTRY 60

May 19, 2020
Naimah Baptiste, 32 years old
New Jersey

No hashtags please,

This is not written to appease,

Parents teach your kids please,

About the birds and bees

So, it doesn't fall on me.

Telling our kids to do what is right

Only to turn around and start a fight!

Less yelling and screaming

Ask your child how they are feeling

How are they dealing... with life?

Too busy for conversation,

But brothers are trying to save the nation,

Start with your home.

Scrolling, searching for the newest trend,

Sisters, your babies crying, not trying to offend,

Being content starts from within.

Fall back, take a moment... and look at what you're hiding from.

ENTRY 61

May 20, 2020
Naimah Baptiste, 32 years old
New Jersey

She tried her best to be truthful,

He tried his best to be just,

She tried her best to be righteous,

He tried his best to be virtuous,

She tried her best to be noble,

He tried his best to be proper,

She tried her best to be respectable,

He tried his best to be irreproachable,

Not a bad word was ever spoken of the chaste, honorable couple.

May we be inspired...

May Allah(swt) give us Jannahtul Firdous.[138] Ameen.

---

138   The highest level in heaven

ENTRY 62

May 20, 2020
Aamila Sameem, 24 years old
Sri Lanka

Perpetuation of massacre

From western to eastern world.

From the States to the Kingdom.

When'll the generosity surpass the cruelty?

Protraction of trauma

On youngsters to infants.

What harm did the infants do?

What's the harm made by the youngsters?

When'll humanity outstrip the brutality?

February, the shortest month of the year,

Remarks the catastrophic death of Ahmaud.

May, the month of awareness,

Interposes between existence and calamity.

Aya's tragic death's a stark reminder,

Islamophobia is alive in the western world.

Whilst the easterners are exasperated with adversity.

The blessed month's embellished by chaos.

And shakes the existence of the people.

When'll this transgress the norms of the philosophy of the

murders?

I endure the modern lynching as ungovernable.

Yet, it's unabated and nurtured by the heretics.

And pauses the grim reality of modernity.

ENTRY 63

May 21, 2020
Naimah Baptiste, 32 years old
New Jersey

The melody danced through the air tickling my heart with a feather,

The tones plunged into my bones vibrating me to the core.

The tune lifted me to the sky removing all thoughts from my mind.

There was no resistance or skirmish,

I completely yield and succumb to the peace.

ENTRY 64

May 22, 2020
Naimah Baptiste, 32 years old
New Jersey

Dear Sister,

This Ramadan you would've been sad we were in quarantine and unable to go to the masjid. I know that Ramadan is your favorite time of year. I missed your smile and the way your kind eyes light up will always be in my heart. How did you manage to always smile and love even when people showed you their ugliest face? You smiled even when you yourself were having a bad day? I miss you. I love you. I don't know if I ever told you? It saddens me to think I never expressed my real love for you in words. But, Alhamduillah I am grateful that I expressed my love through actions. I didn't know you were sick. I took you for granted. I'm sorry. I'm sorry, I wasn't a better friend. I'm sorry, I didn't come see you in the hospital. They wouldn't let me. I'm sorry, I'm stuck in the house because of COVID-19. I really wanted to pray Janaza Salah for you. I'm sorry. Please forgive me. May Allah give us Jannah and grant us to be neighbours in Jannah. Inshallah I will see you again. Ameen.

Love you always.

ENTRY 65

May 22, 2020
Aamila Sameem, 24 years old
Sri Lanka

The month is passing like a bolt of silvery lightning.

And we're here at the verge of bidding it farewell.

I rewind the memories of last Ramadan,[139]

Where I was accompanied by gaiety.

The day is passing swift like a Black Marlin

And we're to bid farewell.

These brooding covetous eyes of mine yearn to stay like
Nightjar, to seek the best out of this month.

They are puffy from sleeplessness.

Yet, the soul's embedded with Kalamullah.[140]

The hour is passing like the blink of an eye,

Where we are dwindling the sins away from us

To welcome our new born selves from the darkness of the
soul into the light.

The minute is passing nimbly like a Peregrine Falcon,

Where my thoughts flip from the present to

When my mother used to make cookies,

And conceal them from us to be served on the day of Eid.

My conscience making me realize how I used to be

With my siblings around.

---

139   The holy month where Muslims fast
140   Word of God

A cherished memory, one I'll never be able to revisit.

Yet, I'm still.

The wind of change hit harder on the human race,

To change the course from north to south and east to west.

And from south to north and west to east.

Where the people are deprived of assembly,

Yet permitted to mirth and contend in seclusion.

Adorn your cage of "quarantine festive" with the memories
of the past.

Inculcate the seeds of happiness on the day of Eid,

And you'll witness an enormous jollity of yourself on the
blessed day.

ENTRY 66

May 23, 2020
Aamila Sameem, 24 years old
Sri Lanka

Black is just a color.

I repeat,

black is just a color equivalent to white.

Repeat after me,

It's the color of the human race.

Minneapolis drenched in oppression,

The plague of racism infested

In the minds of the saviors of the state.

I can't breathe

Floyd beseeched

I repeat,

I can't breathe

Floyd begged.

Repeat after me,

I could breathe only through black and white, together.

Has the States forgotten the history of the presidents?

Or Has the States re-emerged through oppression?

Obama, the known "First African-American" president.

The states rejoiced during his term.

Has it forgotten that black lives exist now after his term is complete?

Does it hinder the resurgence of oppression in the hands of

the White?

Has America abandoned its roots?

Has it set course in a new direction?

Because the wind gusts the breath away in the midst of the public in Minneapolis.

The White supremacy regained its consciousness of discrimination

While the Blacks Collided to the earth by the brutal hands of an escort.

Everything hurts.

Floyd pleaded.

I repeat,

"Everything in the world with color hurts."

Repeat after me,

The world murders the black to crown the "White supremacy."

The dividends among people

Stabilize the world through

discrimination.

When choking is accepted in the light

Then, where's the justice, which is everyone's right?

Justice isn't a chant for Black lives

Yet, it's a chant for humanity.

Summon the humans

to poise the world free from racism.

Summon the humanitarians

to sign the peace treaty today!

Lockdown

Violence is no answer to violence.

Yet, justice existing in peace is the unfeigned victory.

ENTRY 67

May 24, 2020
Kashmir Maryam, 30 years old
Philadelphia

Today I bask in blessings. If I counted them, I would not truly be able to enumerate them. That being said, I feel a time will soon come where the luxuries I currently enjoy will cease, and I will be grasped by a period of struggle and strife. And for some reason, I feel that time is near.

As Ramadan has come to a close, I feel the tranquility that I felt in that blessed month has been lifted, and now negative forces encircle me.

If I have learned anything over the years, it is that Allah's *sunnah* is that He will never disappoint the believing servants, and indeed, Allah has never ever disappointed me in the least.

The night seems blacker now, as if it carries more secrets, but the dawn will always follow. It is only a matter of time. And time is a matter—a meter by which all truths will come to light. Until all those who are oppressed will soon find retribution. Until good will see its results. Until bad will see its end.

Patience, patience, Maryam. A beautiful patience.

ENTRY 68

May 27, 2020
Haala Marikar, 19 years old
Sri Lanka

Some seconds into the video of Ahmaud Arbery's lynching,
I stopped watching,
Because I had the luxury of moving
On to something else
When that distressed me.
When I saw pictures of George Floyd and the headlines that
accompanied those pictures,
I didn't watch the videos at all,
Because I had the luxury of moving
On to something else,
When that distressed me.
When I saw pictures of Breonna Taylor,
They were pictures of a smiling woman holding a bouquet
of yellow flowers in a blue uniform, with the American flag
behind her.
I didn't want to read the details of her death
So I hesitated
Because I had the luxury of moving
On to something else,
When that distressed me.
When I saw Christian Cooper's video of Amy Cooper
talking

On her cell phone, calling
The cops, I was scared of what might come next,
So I scrolled past,
Because I had the luxury of moving
On to something else
When that distressed me.

Ahmaud Arbery didn't have that luxury. Breonna Taylor didn't. George Floyd didn't. Christian Cooper and all the black men and women like him have to live with the knowledge that they could be gunned down, targeted, lynched, any moment, for nothing. They have to tell their kids how to stay safe. They have to be on guard when they're jogging, when they're bird-watching, when they're driving, when they're LIVING IN THEIR OWN HOMES.
I have the luxury of scrolling past, moving on.
They don't.

ENTRY 69

May 27, 2020
Aishah Alam, 31 years old
New York

As I went into social media my sight was flooded with the name George Floyd.

I remember just a few days ago before this new event how I was thinking about the book, *To Kill A Mockingbird* by Harper Lee.

A book about a mild natured man's pursuit of justice on behalf of a falsely accused black man and how this man, who hated confrontation, sat all night with a gun outside the cell of the man he would defend in court so that man would be safe from the brutality of those who wanted to see him dead for no other reason but the color of his skin.

How much has really changed since then?

For nine minutes George Floyd pleaded for his life, cries of breathlessness, ignored by men who call themselves men who pinned him to the ground with their knees on his neck.

It is chilling how history repeats and these cries sounded much like the cries of Eric Garner not too long ago who too said, "I can't breathe, I can't breathe."

I wonder how many mild natured people will be willing to stand up for those who cannot stand up for themselves.

In truth I think that we are a lot braver than we know. That we are more capable of being a means to good than we think. That these circumstances of wrongs will make us speak what is right, even if it goes against our mild natures. I have seen it.

Quiet voices through the frost of loud ones supporting the ones with no voices at all.

It is easy to get lost in that frost. That contradicts the truth of heat as it passes through the media and then the trend goes cold but just because it is cold will we forget? Will I forget?

I pray we can go beyond trends and remember the truth even more when it is stifled, even if we are too scared to say it, even if it goes against our very DNA. I pray Allah gives us the strength to be the true strong believers like Abu Bakr,[141] another mild natured man who gave everything he had for the cause of Islam and even more so when it was a rarity and not yet dominant in the region of its birth.

May we too be the messengers of the messenger[142] in calling to truth and justice. Ameen.

---

141 A companion, and through his daughter, father-in-law of Prophet Muhammad

142 Refers to Muhammad, the last messenger of Islam

ENTRY 70

May 28, 2020
Asna Khan, 19 years old
India

"Why us?"
 I remember asking my father
As he lay with a bullet in his throat
Tears making me choke
Blood on his favorite coat.
A short, sharp breath was all I heard
As his fingers curled around the toy
That he promised his little boy.
I still wait for his final word.
For years.
For years I thought I had killed my father.
I've learnt to live
With a knee on my neck,
The bullet in my chest.
In a castle of dust,
Their looks of disgust.
And their words like poison sting
Wrapped in flowers of spring.
I've learnt to live
On an empty, stormy shore
Halting at the footsteps of my door
Turing back to my wife,

My child, my life,
"Goodbye."
Flashbacks from my past
This could be my last.
Today, the headlines flash again.
Another loss, another blame
Fuel to a raging flame
But I know they'll forget his name.
What would they do if every alley, every path
screams the names of those they've killed?
What would they do if their rivers flowed
with the blood they've spilled?
Many graveyards I've seen fill up with my own.
Does not our final breath chill them to their bone?
Our blood is scattered, sunken in this soil.
And I hear every grain as it speaks.
It pleads, screams
Buries shattered dreams.
In the quiet of the night
A whisper rises from beneath,
"I can't breathe."
Curtains down,
I've been in darkness, drowning in the air.
Footsteps mix with cries of my own,
They run, grow louder.
I silence the talking stone.
Small hands wrap themselves around my neck.

Lockdown

Tears make her choke, another shipwreck.
"Why us, daddy?" she asks me.
Thunder in a stormy sea.
I have no words.
And the air gets stuck in my throat.
It feels like death, my final breath
So I clutch my father's coat.
Colored.
Watered.
Lies.
Darkness in my eyes.
"I can't breathe."
And I'm not the only one.

ENTRY 71

May 31, 2020
Haala Marikar, 19 years old
Sri Lanka

Please, don't talk to me
About the Statue of Liberty.
Don't you dare tell me
America is the land of the free.
No, wait, yes, I agree,
America is the land of the free,
But conditionally.
America is the land of the free
IF you're White.
America is the land of the free,
If you blind yourself
To the crimes
Of your system.
America is the land of the free
If you're a White woman
Who can fake distress on a phone call
To the cops
and threaten
An African-American
And get away with it.
America is the land of the free,
If you're a White man

Lockdown

With a truck and a gun and White friends
Who'll help you end
The life of a Black man
Who went jogging.
America is the land of the free,
If you're a White man
In a blue uniform
Who will press his knee
Against a black man's neck
And ignore his pleas
Of "I can't breathe, man, I can't breathe."
America is the land of the free,
Conditionally.

ENTRY 72

May 31, 2020
Alma Salam, 21 years old
Sri Lanka

There were many left behind with so many untold stories. Where they couldn't raise their voices because fear was overwhelming. Why didn't people realize that everyone in the human body is the same except the melanin concentration in their bodies!

What makes you feel that you have to condemn the Black? What thoughts convinced you that you are the superior? Who taught you and showed you? Didn't you have the capability of deciphering bad from good? Did you have the right to take a life?

Who gave you the authority?

Why didn't you have fear when the public was watching you? Was it that easy to tackle them? What made you do this?

So many questions. Why, what, who? So many questions gathered in my mind. Why, why, why? Did people matter? During this time of the pandemic where people had the urge to save lives. Displaying the death tolls on huge screens. When the whole world was inventing more simplified devices for ventilation, why didn't you hear the voice saying, "I CAN'T BREATHE?"

chapter Four

June 2020

COVID-19 worldwide statistics
for June 2020:[143]

New cases at the start of the month: 100389
New deaths at the start of the month: 3007

New cases at the end of the month: 174925
New deaths at the end of the month: 5710

143 Source: The New York Times

ENTRY 73

June 1, 2020
Aishah Alam, 31 years old
New York

Lockdown phase one begins in a week—NEW YORK IS REOPENING!

These are unprecedented times.

This sounds like a cliche, like I have heard this phrase repeated before, but never have I seen a time like this.

Though I am limited by so many factors—my age, where I live, the circles I am in, the things I choose to be exposed to.

What a world we live in right now: a virus that has spread and become a pandemic, quarantined in our homes—the rich and the poor, wearing masks and keeping six feet from one another—as if another part of our connection to one another has ended.

Just a few days ago, a few weeks ago, three unnecessary deaths due to that old foe, that ancient pride coined by none other than the devil himself. Now we leave our homes to protest racism.

We are angry, despite the color of our skin, and we want justice for the victims. The most recent being George Floyd, a 46 year old Black man who was suffocated to death under the knee of a White police man who could not hide his absolute contempt towards him. For nine minutes he clamped his knee on this nonresistant man's neck, even though that man slowly died whispering that he could not breathe. The words are hauntingly similar to the words of Eric Garner, but it was not done to copy him, it was not done for any other reason except begging for his life.

Begging.

And now people have left their homes to protest.

Just moments ago, at 8:30ish p.m., we got a city wide amber alert stating that NY would be on curfew from 11 p.m. till 5 a.m.

Lefrak city, just down my street, is boarded up and police are stopping non-residents from going in.

Just a few minutes after my sister went shopping in Philly, the store got raided—her son, a toddler, was with her.

Burn racism. Burn the oppression, the systematic and repetitive institutionalized racism.

ENTRY 74

June 3, 2020
Aishah Alam, 31 years old
New York

I wanted to write more in the previous entry but I was not able to.

Today I got another notification that New York is under curfew, this time from 8 p.m. because of the raids.

In addition, there have been tornado threats—in Philly, of all places!

First the virus, then the lockdown, then the racist killings, then the protests, and now the storms.

Everything seems to be building up to something.

People are tired and they are angry, this is why they are burning things. But fire can never bring peace.

It only roars and spreads and is hasty with no organization, only a pattern of rage with no thought as it tears down any sanity one has.

And the fire is spreading, lit by the racist, lit by the pride, lit. And it is being flamed by those who oppose the wrong, but their way is also fire.

And what do fire and fire make? More fire.

Only water can bring the roar down.

And it is raining down, it is raining from the eyes of those who cry for the dead of an innocent.

And with these tears, some of us are waking up.

Some of our hearts are waking us.

This entry is like my mind, all over the place. I end with this verse which helps me contextualize everything:

"And (remember) when We said to the angels: 'Prostrate unto Adam.' They prostrated except Iblis (Satan). He said: 'Shall I prostrate to one whom You created from clay?'" (Quran 17:61).

It brings me peace because Allah knows. He knows everything.

ENTRY 75

June 4, 2020
Aamila Sameem, 24 years old
Sri Lanka

The sight of the infant

Disturbed the Black mother.

Why does the baby roll his eyes?

And Black mom heard the poignant voice of the newborn.

"Mommy, will I be a burden to this gruesome world?

Will I be tortured for my color?"

The Black mother startled after hearing the questions,

Where she was left with no answer.

Yet, a series of questions interrogated.

"Mommy, will I be defeated by the injustices of this world?

Will my innocence be taken for granted by this world?"

After every pause, she heard a voice sobbing,

And it was from a Black mother.

The questions proposed in the deepest core of the new Black mother,

Not from the newborn

Suggesting the internal trauma of the Black parents of the world.

What made her snivel and sob at the sight of the baby?

Is it the world?

Or

Is it the modern "trending" injustices?

Lockdown

Indeed! The injustices that are clouded in the world
Generated the new mom to explore a safe shield to guard
her newborn.
Mother's thoughts perpendicularly dipped to the violation
of human rights.
And the repercussion of Floyd's murder is no more under
the control of the "White mainstream."
And her thoughts absconded to an autistic brother's murder
in Palestine.
And police brutality in Sri Lanka where an autistic boy,
Thariq, was assaulted.
Is racism amalgamated with color and religion too?
And she contemplated, a thudding sound reverberated in-
side her heart,
Where's the justice for the people?
Where's the justice for the innocent?
Who's primed to save the human lives from danger,
If saviors are transformed into lynchers?
This isn't the psyche of the new Black mother,
It's the voices that aren't raised against the "unique" injus-
tices of the world!

ENTRY 76

June 5, 2020
Haala Marikar, 19 years old
Sri Lanka

When the riots are over
And the streets have cleared,
Remember, there's still voices
That need to be heard.

When you get back home
And you put down your signs,
Remember Syria, remember Kashmir,
Remember Palestine.

When you go back to posting
Everyday stuff on your feed,
Remember the Uyghurs,
The Rohingya, the Yemenis.

When the roads are empty,
And the placards are gone,
Remember, there's still much
More work to be done.

When the slogans are dropped
And the hashtags have changed,

Lockdown

Remember, there is
Still so much we must change.

ENTRY 77

June 6, 2020
Asna Khan, 19 years old
India

I walk down the empty streets,

My tears walk with me,

A lone sound.

My footsteps on the ground,

They set my fears free.

Aisles of shattered hearts,

In the mirror do I see,

Each piece cries,

Tells a different tale,

Sings a different plea.

I stare at the mirror,

At who I ought to be.

I am Safoora Zargar.

Muslim.

I spoke up for justice,

For peace.

For injustice to cease.

I now sit in a dark corner of an Indian prison.

Longing to feel the heartbeats of my baby.

Will I be blessed with the first cry?

I pray my baby doesn't die.

I am Iyad Halak, 32.

Lockdown

Palestinian.

Autistic.

On my way to school,

A toy in my hand.

They screamed at me. I ran.

I heard them fire three.

Their hate pierced me.

I am Thariq Ahamad, 14.

Muslim.

Autistic.

They pushed me off my bicycle,

Beat me up, tortured me.

I could only weep,

But the scars on my body speak.

They say those like me kill.

A 6 year-old's skill?

I am Shukri Abdi, 12.

Black.

"They're always mean to me. They don't like me."

I had a heart, feelings.

Still hurts, bleeding.

It was hate that killed another Muslim daughter.

I heard their laughter as I drowned underwater.

I am Julius Jones.

Black.

"I have spent the past 20 years on death row for a crime I did not commit,

Did not witness,

And was not at."

The clock ticks.

One-hundred and twenty two days.

Darkness.

Death to dawn's rays.

I am one of the 14 Afghans.

A refugee.

I love my home, my Kabul jan,

Yet I was forced to flee.

Left the bombs behind my back,

Just to die a brutal death.

I felt the fire devour my skin until my final breath.

I am the Uyghur,

Stripped of my religion.

I am Palestinian,

Killed for who I am.

I am Yemeni,

Dying of hunger.

I am Syrian,

Bombed on my own land.

I am Afghan,

War tearing me apart.

I am Kashmiri,

My blood tills the sand.

I am Black,

Hate chokes me,

Lockdown

I can't breathe.
I am Muslim,
I make their poisons seethe.
I am Asna Khan.
Indian.
Afghan.
I read to you these words,
These words have failed me.
Every heart the mirror shows,
Pleads to be heard,
Pleads to be free.
I pray I don't fail them.

ENTRY 78

June 6, 2020
Nameera Fatima, 16 years old
India

O you the believer of Allah,
Take a deep breath, zeal your imaan.
Stand up with your powerful weapon.
Add some essence to your worship.
And verily, dua[144] is the essence of worship,
That brings you closer to your creator.

O you the believer of Allah,
So proudly you say, "I am of the Muminun."[145]
Then why are these powerful weapons not strong enough,
To help you against those who resist faith.
To help you against those who oppress you.
To help you against those who aim to put you down.

O you the believer of Allah,
Defy the resistor who resists you by the remembrance of the Almighty God.
Increase your faith, your hope towards The ultimate recourse.
Ask Allah to change the quandaries you are facing today,
Ask Allah to heal you, to guide you and to keep you firm in Taqwa.[146]

---

144   Prayer
145   Believer
146   Islamic term for being conscious and cognizant of God

ENTRY 79

June 6, 2020
Naimah Baptiste, 32 years old
New Jersey

Death of a friend,

Is sadness that draws upon you the darkest hours.

When the room is still and the world sleeps,

The reminder is heavy in your chest,

The tears behind your eyes aggravated that they cannot make their way out.

The soul that rises from your body looms over its home.

Dreams of a friend,

The loss,

No goodbye,

No preparation.

Death of a friend,

Longing to see her again but not wanting to die.

ENTRY 80

June 7, 2020
Aamila Sameem, 24 years old
Sri Lanka

Let the love bemuse you

Let the compassion attract you

Let the kindness cover you

Yet, don't contemplate about the complexion

Whether its White, Black or Brown

It's the color of the human race

Bestowed by God's grace

Will you complain?

Will you discriminate?

Will you fight for the color?

Yet, the choice lies at your feet.

Where you can choose between the two.

Fighting for the color

Or standing against injustices.

A simple note at the end

Would bring forth a greater change.

ENTRY 81

June 7, 2020
Aamila Sameem, 24 years old
Sri Lanka

Black a color
divide
the human race
into two hemispheres.
One for
White supremacy.
And the other for
Black lives.
World,
a strange place
seeks the color
to define the human race.

ENTRY 82

June 8, 2020
Haala Marikar, 19 years old
Sri Lanka

This picture, a painting of my father's, had me reflecting upon how these two colours, black and white, are equally contributing to the beauty of the image as a whole. Had this been entirely white, or entirely black, there would be no image to it at all.

It led me to think about deeper issues that we are facing today.

"And among His Signs is the creation of the heavens and the earth, and the difference of your languages and colours. Verily, these are indeed signs for men of sound knowledge" (Quran 30:22).

How ignorant we are that we choose to discriminate against people based on the colour of their skin, when this is indeed one of the signs of the Greatness of The Creator!

Every time we think of ourselves as better than someone else based on the colour of their skin, every time we recommend a fairness cream to a girl of a darker complexion, we need to remind ourselves of this.

Bilal (may Allah be pleased with him) was a freed black slave, and he was the first caller to prayer and one of the greatest friends of the Prophet Muhammad (peace be upon him), and of the most devoted Muslims. Zaid ibn Haritha, the adopted son of the Prophet Muhammad (peace be upon him), was black. Umm Ayman, who took care of the Prophet Muhammed (peace be upon him) and who was described as his second mother, was black. Usama bin Zaid, Sa'ad Al Aswad, Ammar bin Yasir (may Allah be pleased with them) were all Black companions of the Prophet Muhammed (peace be upon him) and were amongst the most God-fearing men, who endured much for and contributed much to the cause of Islam.

Salman el Farisi (may Allah be pleased with him) was Persian. Abu Hurayra (may Allah be pleased with him) was Yemeni.

There are so many more examples of people of different races and colours and countries, being of the most devoted Muslims in the time of the Prophet Muhammed (peace be upon him), and they were indeed of his dearest companions.

Islam teaches us the beauty in diversity in this hadith of the Prophet Muhammed (peace be upon him):

"O people, your Lord is one and your father Adam is one. There is no favor of an Arab over a foreigner, nor a foreigner over an Arab, and neither white skin over black skin, nor black skin over white skin, except by righteousness" (Source: Musnad Ahmad 22978).

We must see the beauty in the glistening ebony of

someone's skin, in the beautiful bronze, in the warm browns, in the pinks, in the whites, in the yellows. We must see colour, and we must see the beauty in it. We have all been created in different colors, shapes, sizes... and different is beautiful.

ENTRY 83

June 10, 2020
Naimah Baptiste, 32 years old
New Jersey

I'm not just a teacher or a glorified babysitter for some. I have been tasked with creating curriculums, educating students to proficiency, in addition to shaping their delicate minds. My goal is to promote normal functioning members of society who do not compromise their morals.

After reading the novel *Wonder* by RJ Palacio, most students were inspired to create their own class precept. My favorite precept was:

"I have a voice. My voice is strong. My voice can change the world" (7G, 2017-2018).

It's amazing how one phrase can motivate a group of young minds. They began to leave their own little imprints within our school (through events on bullying and childhood diabetes, and by participating on sports teams) and outside of our school during Debate Team tournaments (we made it to Nationals!).

To all my students from that class:

Even though many will try to tear you down, remember you're a pillar of hope, strength and elegance. You are a strong Muslim woman. Your color or decree can never define you. You create positive change. You break down barriers and educate all within your path.

ENTRY 84

June 10, 2020
Awesome Imam, 20 years old
Nigeria

INJUSTICE!

My dream is a day to come.

For it I'll wait dusks and dawns.

Or maybe for a twilight to show

A sign of a different sunrise I've not known.

My dream is a day to come

Where all humans are seen as the same.

Where Islam is attached to the Muslims

And not a fear, not ISLAMOPHOBIA.

My dream is a day to come

Where black and white aren't used to describe humans.

Then Islam,

Known for its meaning, peace.

My dream is a day to come.

My dream, my day,

My dream is a day of JUSTICE.

Lockdown

June 12, 2020
Aamila Sameem, 24 years old
Sri Lanka

I see hearts and smiles

blended with fake identity.

And moulded with wickedness

and carrying the ravishing thoughts.

I see shaking hands in vanity.

And trespassing the norms.

While holding the unexplainable darkness.

I see warm hugs and kisses

coinciding with jealousy.

And clenching the knife for a "friendly stab."

I see texts in vibrant color

colliding with supreme compassion.

While withholding the darkest secrets in the tiny part of the

body.

I see coruscating faces

credited with applause

and succeeding in the "drama" on the stage.

While their "real" life is an "unsolved mystery movie."

I've adopted "Myself"

to learn and lean,

to tie and untie,

to scythe and writhe,

from the darkest reality of the human psyche.

The undeniable ties

integrated "Myself" to escort a "lethargic" life.

While concealing the crepuscular truth about the human race.

ENTRY 86

June 14, 2020
Aishah Alam, 31 years old
New York

It's 11:20 p.m. and we are stranded in Philly.

My one-month-old is with me and my 19-month-old. It is completely desolate around me in this gas station.

My brother tried to pump air into the tire and he ended up popping it and now it's completely ruined so here we are, waiting. Waiting and waiting for a guy called Darnell to come and fix it. We have been waiting for HOURS!

Wow. This is truly a test of patience.

It's so easy to talk about patience but when you are in a situation with two children under two and family who know exactly what NOT to say in this situation, here comes the pokes from the devil along with actual mosquito bites. Add the post-apocalyptic climate where my mask is buried deep in some place in my bag, in the back seat, of which the doors won't open.

Breathe in. Breathe out. Didn't work.

Not only that, but the riots sparked by the death of George Floyd are still raging here and places are boarded up, decorated with spray stating, "cleared up" and "empty."

We are not completely alone here. There are two girls whose tire is also flat, and my brother is helping them out while we wait. Oh, the irony.

My brother is also going to every person who turns into the gas station and asking if they are Darnell and they shake their head politely and drive away like a beast on fire. I would be creeped out a little too, to be honest.

Oh look, there's two deer that just walked in front of the gas station!

I've never seen a deer in person.

On that note, what have I learnt from all of this?

I have no patience. Well, nothing compared to what I thought I had.

Anyway, I have to preserve my battery, I only have 18%.

May Allah give us patience, ameen.

ENTRY 87

June 15, 2020
Aamila Sameem, 24 years old
Sri Lanka

The whole world is busy treating Covid 19,

while some nations treating other nations

through violence and injustice.

The world did fail to invent the vaccine.

Yet, it endorses the nation using artilleries.

The world failed to treat 500 thousand infected people.

Yet, the world praises the injustices.

The world is conquered through darkness.

And failed to accommodate the light.

The dark clouds veiled humanity

from the cold hearts.

And unleashed the gruesome tactics upon the human.

The world did fail to treat the injustices.

As the world failed to treat the pathogen.

When will the world learn its lesson?

How will they encourage the patients to be patient with the
undeniable scenario of modernity?

ENTRY 88

June 16, 2020
Naimah Baptiste, 32 years old
New Jersey

Careful love, your mask is slipping low.

The hate speech you teach is contagious you know.

You will infect the youth and their clean impressionable minds.

Stay six feet in front or six feet behind.

Nevermind, just leave! There is no place for you.

No one wants your high feverish glow,

No one wants your black speckled heart growing slowly to pitch,

No one wants uncontrollable coughing, squeezing, wheezing, you've dug your ditch.

So keep your assimilation to yourself

So keep your cunning nationalism to yourself

So keep your racial slurs to yourself

So keep your witty prejudice jokes to yourself

No thanks

It's urine in the ear

Allah is the master of all and the equalizer of everything

You are a test!

Careful love, your mask is slipping low.

ENTRY 89

June 16, 2020
Naimah Baptiste, 32 years old
New Jersey

My saliva filled up my mouth drooling over the juicy piece,
tantalizing, succulent, mouthwatering savory sweet meat,
The luscious taste and grinding down awakened my senses,
the texture was delectable with the right amount of crisp that
my heart fluttered and my stomach yearned for more
and I indulged...
She screamed out in pain as my knife carved her flesh from
the bone.
My eyes widened, the metallic ironic smell filled the air.
The sweet meat turned to ash in my mouth.
The dry rotting flesh was stuck in my teeth,
White maggots oozed from my mouth.
I picked up hot embers to kill the maggots.
My fingers were blacked and singed.
My tongue cauterized by my own scorched hand trying to
remove the dead flesh and maggots from my once beautiful
face crafted by our creator.
I bowed my head down and raised my hands.
Ya Allah please forgive me for back biting,
I didn't realize the extent of my cannibalistic behavior.

ENTRY 90

June 16, 2020
Naimah Baptiste, 32 years old
New Jersey

Satisfied—by superficial allowances: movies, news anchors,
TV shows, murals, protests

Laws remain the same

Lack of education

Low socioeconomic status

Less opportunity

Police Brutality

Poor Justice Systems

Rise in single parent households

The success story of the exception but replayed as the rule

Outraged by the blatant brutality, daily deaths and rampant
racism.

Satisfied—by superficial allowances: movies, news anchors,
TV shows, murals, protests.

ENTRY 91

June 16, 2020
Naimah Baptiste, 32 years old
New Jersey

No justice no peace....
No peace of mind
No peace for the body
No peace for the soul
No piece of the Apple pie
No piece of the wealth
No piece in law creation
Ya Allah, I want Justice and Peace. Ameen.

ENTRY 92

June 16, 2020
Naimah Baptiste, 32 years old
New Jersey

Heavy, burdened with hate.

Years of trauma resurface.

Rewatching, rewinding, replaying has been a gateway.

I enter in the blank numbness of dark.

Hurting so deeply... numbness is a relief of mental and emotional pain.

Deafening silence in black endless, numbness.

I open my eyes and let go.

ENTRY 93

June 17, 2020
Naimah Baptiste, 32 years old
New Jersey

"I should've fed you to the hogs when I had a chance." Her words spat at him.

He was broken.
At the side of a broken nowhere
In a broken country,
He was born in a broken village
with broken homes,
He came into this world unimportant, unwanted, unloved,
but She, felt obligated.
She, would break him intentionally or not.

Broken only breaks.

Left under the house to play he stacked sticks,
Left under the house, he built,
Soon She left! So he was forgotten,
Left under the house, broken.
Left, with the man that he was told was his father,
Shamelessly, he had the nerve to share the face of a neighbor down the street.
Born to two broad noses and kinky coiled people,

His nose was pointed and hair pin straight.

A bastard.

Hated by Her. A secret broken. Now revealed.

For he was unwanted.

He did not know love, he was hated.

He did not know kindness, he learnt cruelty.

Left! She went away to a new lover,

Left! Old secrets behind,

Left! With Her husband,

Left! The last thought on her mind.

He was left with "father."

Broken only breaks.

Hardened and broken he left.

He left the drunken rage of his "father."

He left the drunken rants of his "father."

He left the drunken tears of his "father."

He left the drunken cries of his "father."

Broken only breaks.

Fueled with rage burnt to success,

He was self-sufficient.

Fueled with hurt molded to be unstoppable,

He was self-sufficient.

Lockdown

Hopeful.
She naively came along with eyes of kindness,
Hopeful.
She could mend this broken,
Hopeful.
To share her love,

Broken only brakes.

Broken, broke their marriage.
Broken, broke their love.
Broken, broke her soul leant to heal.
Broken, broke the kids.

Broken only breaks.

Broken, broke more than he could fix.
He left broken, his wife.
He left broken, his home.
He left broken, his kids.
He left broken, the possibility they built.

Broken only breaks.

He broke his daughters' faith in man.
He broke his daughters' faith in men.

Broken only the brakes.

He tries again, less broken this time.
He builds and breaks down, one more time.
He builds and breaks down, another time.
He builds and breaks down, one more time.
He tries again, less broken this time...
Broken, please have peace of mind...

Broken, she no longer haunts you,
She is no longer there.
Open your heart,
And do not fear.
She's hurt you so bad that no words can give you ease,
But, Allah has blessed you, with the best of decrees.
All your past wives they love you so,
They teach their children peace and love, you know.
There is no malice or hatred you see.
That woman broke you and it's plain to see.
She did not love you or give you the kindness you deserved,
But look around at the blessings from up above.

Allah has given you mercy,
Allah has given you mercy,
Allah has given you mercy,

A kind wife, that loves you beyond all relief.
Over ten children and most of whom are on the deen,

Lockdown

Establishing salah for the Siraatal Mustaqeem.[147]
We raise our hands in Du'a to Allah, for your soul.
All we want is for you to be whole.

We know that She hurt you so bad,
And in turn that has made you merciless, miserable, mad.
But, when melancholy meets sadness,
Remember, that you have surpassed all that madness.

Allah has surrounded you with so much love
That your neighbors are jealous of the blessings from up
above.
So, do not use your speech saying ill things from your face,
Use language that uplifts your children with grace,
Your eldest stands tall, a little broken too, but she knows you
love her and you have done the best you can do.
Your second in line, is still hurting and it's plain to see,
 she questions why she wasn't good enough for you, to be
the man that she needed you to be.
Your third in line, holds you at arm's length, aware not to
get too close,
living in fear of your unpredictable reproach.
Your fourth in line, is there and wants to be loved too,
open your arms wide for her too.
Your fifth in line is strong and efficient, her work ethic's
proficient. She buries herself in work, not to feel the pain.

---

147   The straight path

But all you do is give her the blame.

Your sixth in line, missed out, perhaps because her mother was smart to get out.

Your seventh in line, is your first son, whom you expect to be perfect.

But remember, Allah created children with parents for guidance. Show that boy some kindness.

Your eighth in line, is all smiles and ready to learn.

Make sure you don't break him when you're ready to burn.

Your last little three, unscathed by your brutality.

You see, they are the ones who have something special, the possibility,

of a whole person, being all that he is meant to be.

Time and time again we will help you along the way,

Alhamduillah, your behavior has not caused us to go astray.

We are all love and kindness you see

We are forever bonded, forever ruled by our commonality,

Being broken is a choice and so is love.

Choose us this time because She is gone.

You are no longer in her shadows, she no longer lurks in yours.

You are free and unburdened from the oppression that was yours.

Allow Us into your heart for all of our sakes.

Please, un-break your subconscious cycle of hate.

ENTRY 94

June 18, 2020
Aishah Alam, 31 years old
New York

Is it June 18th already? I really wanted to write what happened after that night we were stranded.

One thing which stood out to me on the way home was the crescent moon. No cliche. It was so close to the world I couldn't stop looking at it all the way home. We waited from 8 p.m. until 1 a.m. for the car mechanic to arrive and thank God my babies were sleeping.

The two ladies whose car also broke down— not only with a flat tire like us, but a flat tire on the same side as ours— stayed with us until they knew we were ok.

I don't believe in coincidences. We are in an empty gas station in the middle of nowhere and two cars break down in the exact same way.

My mum, who was sitting in the front seat, then asked if they had read the Quran.[148] I couldn't believe it when one of the girls said she was Muslim!

The other one said she believed in God and was a poet. I felt an instant connection with both of them.

The poet had a one-year-old daughter and the father of her daughter had died when she was pregnant. She was

---

148   The holy book of guidance for Muslims

only 20 when he passed away.

When the men came to fix the tire, they came in two pick-up trucks and I remember my heart beating like crazy.

I guess I have watched too many movies. But when I asked my brother later what he thought, he said he felt like it was something out of the movie *The Purge*.

When the door opened, I sat up and then two men came out of the truck.

It's crazy, the fact that one man had a beard, and both were African American made me feel at ease. I felt even more at ease when the man with a beard greeted us with the Muslim greeting of peace.

It's so funny because we had just been saying how the fact there were Muslims and black people together, was probably a supremacist's worst nightmare (we were in a red zone of Philly).

Finally, the tire was fixed, and the girls said bye and left.

So the trucks and everyone goes and then guess what?

OUR CAR BATTERY WENT DEAD.

No lie.

That could not have been random. My brothers got two jumping cables and called the girls to see if they could jump start us. They came and helped us once again and finally we were on our way again.

Then we get a message from them saying their tire had

not been fitted properly and they had gotten into a crash.

They were ok but the car was badly damaged. I couldn't believe it.

What a night.

Writing this now, I think highly of these two girls. They came out to help us despite the virus, despite the riots, despite not knowing who we were in the middle of nowhere and didn't even think twice before doing it because they saw two babies in the car in the middle of the night and they couldn't turn their backs on us.

Sometimes we think that faith is by our outerwear, how we look, what we say, but truly the matter of faith is between God and you. A big part of faith is shown through what we do and what these two girls did was selfless. It was kind and from the heart. You just don't meet people like that very often.

May their actions bear witness for them on the Day of Judgment and weigh heavily on their scales, ameen.

ENTRY 95

June 18, 2020
Haala Marikar, 19 years old
Sri Lanka

Today, I stared
At a blank page,
And waited for the words to appear.
I waited for the pain in my heart,
And my prayers for my brethren
To manifest themselves in letters and words and sentences
and verse.
I waited for my pen
To rewrite the same old story in different words, again and
again,
War and politics, politics and war,
Until the two words become synonymous with one another.
I waited for my pen
To write my prayers
For Yemen,
That blessed land,
So beloved to the most beloved (peace be upon him),
For Yemen, the land of felicity,
Where my brethren
Starve to death,
Emaciated limbs, and sightless eyes,
And always that story of a little girl

Lockdown

Who put on her Eid clothes and earrings
Before the moon was sighted
Because, "Who knows,"
She said with her wide gap-toothed smile,
"The air raids might come and I might die."

She did die.
Of starvation.
Later.

So my pen rewrites
This story,
Even though it is tired,
Even though I am tired,
Though my heart is heavy,
I realize
What a privilege it is
To feel momentarily sad,
Instead of perpetually scared,
To imagine myself in a warzone
Instead of living in one,
And so I write.

ENTRY 96

June 18, 2020
Aamila Sameem, 24 years old
Sri Lanka

I heard the loudest cry from the eastern world.
I wondered,
And pondered.
The cry shook my existence.

My eyes searched in the scorching sun.
Heard the cry from the eastern world.
The busy world indulged in pandemic,
While the virus plans to delete Yemen from the world map.
I was bewildered and astonished with the cry, making me
realize that I'm a little creature.

The war subjected them to suffer in pain.
And to remain with famine.
The deadly virus left them orphaned,
Alienated from the rest of the world.
My thoughts are cuddled with the cry.

By the fact that Yemenis are deserted.
The cries cracked the silence of the eastern and western
hemispheres.
Yet, no response.

Lockdown

No compassion.

No humanitarian aid.

Yemenis dived deeper into the oceanic water of the pandemic.

And they found no option,

But to accept the reality.

Here I'm sprinkling ink for the love of humanity.

Eyes aren't blind.

Nor are the ears deaf.

Listen and look at the cry.

And raise your hands and pray!

ENTRY 97

June 20, 2020
Aamila Sameem, 24 years old
Sri Lanka

The oozing rainy breeze
embraced the mind
to stop the whining soul
from past memories.
The rationalized mind
evolved from the past
to cuddle the present
to perceive the verities of the world.
A breathtaking scenario
in the eastern world.
Children are left orphans,
Mothers carrying containers,
While the pathogen transfigured to reel ruler.
The real suppressor continues his profession.
I don't see lending ears
Nor visionary eyes.
What I see is lost cinematic soul's video
popping in my Feed.
While Yemenis suffer in Famine.
Does it hinder the futile life of the breathers?

ENTRY 98

June 20, 2020
Nameera Fatima, 16 years old
India

THE BLEEDING PARADISE

There is a place called heaven on the Earth

Where slavery has been right from it's birth.

The people are always succumbed by death.

And you'll find no one there that hasn't ever bled.

The land holds the bodies of our brothers,

Who once used to be the Apple's eye of their mothers.

The fathers couldn't see their bundles of joy

As they fell prey to the conspiracies of the decoy.

The husbands couldn't spend time with their wives,

As they were brutally killed with the bloody knives.

The sisters lost their brothers who once used to be their security,

Now their bodies are lying in impurity.

Seeing this horror everyone shivers.

But there's no one with whom it can be discussed.

There the elegant mountains are always covered with snow.

And the blood in the rivers always flows.

The valleys of this land witness all atrocities.

But their silence keeps on increasing curiosities.

Don't know why Allah made them wait

Hope He has written the best in their fate.

ENTRY 99

June 21, 2020
Awesome Imam, 20 years old
Nigeria

If man were in a single complexion,

Maybe there would be no basis for injustice.

Maybe there would be no lovers of racism.

Maybe there would be no spoilers of the bail system.

If man spoke only a single dialect,

Maybe there would be no need for inferiority select.

Maybe arrests wouldn't be one-sided and violent.

Maybe people wouldn't be judged by their accents.

But these were only the few questions I could find answers to,

'Cause I still think and ask:

Who named one complexion white and the other black?

Who made one higher in status and the other less?

Who gave one more rights over the other?

Where did the complex of inferiority originate from?

'Cause their known difference is their melanin content.

Even in leadership we still find racial grading.

But who should claim a voice looking at melanin deficiency?

Yet we don't,

'Cause we believe in equality.

THE PROBLEM OF THIS GENERATION IS LACK OF

HUMANITY.

STOP!

Stop the killings, the harassing, injustice, inferiority complex, phobia-spreading, using the terms BLACK and WHITE!

'Cause WE, we are tired!

If you insist you don't understand,

If you're trying to make man a single race,

If you are trying to make your language "THE LANGUAGE OF ALL,"

Then I will have no option but to give you more of my poetry.

LET JUSTICE BEGIN!

ENTRY 100

June 22, 2020
Aamila Sameem, 24 years old
Sri Lanka

A tribute to My soul
For being courageous
amidst the chaos in life.
The storm passed
amalgamating the air of worries
and happiness.
Here, I'm turning a year old.
The tornado hit harder
and shook the crust of my life.
Yet, the core melted anxieties
and worries to a yearning Butterfly.
Freedom clutched the "self"
reverberating the waves of defeat
and victories.
Here, I'm turning a year old with
memories of life.
The pen held me
to sketch the thoughts in an array.
And to evolve the planet of hope
through rays.
Years passed,
from whining baby

to winning lady,

to becoming the poet laureate of

her Kingdom.

Stabs and words

infested my soul to bleed in red.

Yet, here I'm bleeding in Ink

to transform the dark world with

an enlightened thought

to linger upon the people and the world!

ENTRY 101

June 25, 2020
Aamila Sameem, 24 years old
Sri Lanka

An airborne pandemic of violence storming Yemen,
Since 2015.
The black spot on humanity blinded many eyes from seek-
ing justice.
Human souls are walking tirelessly.
But no fleshy body.
Only the "human skeleton" walks;
"Humanitarian crisis overwhelmed in Yemen."
Yet, the eyes are blind.
While the ears are deaf.
The blood of injustices flows like a cascade.
And ends up at the verge of crisis.
The policy of blockade refrain Yemenis from surviving.
Left to starve and thirst.
The skeletons step forward to challenge their existence.
The unheard cries smear the black spot.
What are we doing to stop the extinction?
To savages, who fail to provide humanitarian aid, carry the
name of Muslim.
The deadly virus is human
Who hid the compassionate hearts with evilness?
The violence is unleashed.

And the sufferings are unheard.

The world fails to focus the camera.

Yemen has become a blind spot for dispossessed humans

Who seek bloodbaths and violation.

The outrageous pandemic seeks to expunge Yemen from the map.

Who'll win the battle?

Is it Yemenis or pandemic?

The answer is ambiguous.

The calamitous series of attacks from human and nature

beseeches Yemen to fall into the bog of Famine.

The apocalyptic scenario inflicted by wretched creatures

Who ought not to be called human.

Let the world focus the tripod in the direction of

The unheard cries,

The unseen bony bodies.

Let's continue to ink our thoughts to purge the black mark from humanity.

ENTRY 102

June 26, 2020
Aamila Sameem, 24 years old
Sri Lanka

Passion bridged the pen holders
Who're the voice of Islam.
The bridge of "Strangers Poets"[149] reignited the passion
to blaze the ink of cascade to flow with
the mission to create a change in the world.
The light of friendship ignited
from the western to eastern world
affixing through the nerve of writing.
The organization initiated by two beautiful souls
Who carry the alluring names in Islamic history,
The submerged voice of
Uyghur, Yemenis, Rohingya and Syrians raised high.
And the ink dripped to ignite the change
with the power of words and voices.
Here, I'm inking my thoughts
Which heave the existing knowledge
to act as the voice of the Muslim Ummah.[150]
Here, I'm leaving a note of appreciation to those
Who marked the beginning of an exquisite voyage to quench
the thirst for poetry!

---

149 The Strangers Poets was the original name of Strange Inc., the sponsoring nonprofit entity of this project.
150 The whole community of Muslims bound together by ties of religion

ENTRY 103

June 16, 2020
Naimah Baptiste, 32 years old
New Jersey

To all my beloved students,

I want you to know despite all the crazy events that have transpired this year that I am extremely proud of you all.

To my 8th grade girls,

I have had the opportunity to get to know you all very well during our short physical year. I have had the opportunity to teach and befriend you all. You ladies are stronger when you work together and brilliant when you focus. I pray that our lessons remain with you forever and that you never lose the drive and momentum you have now. You can change the world without having to change who you are!

To my 8th grade boys,

I have had most of you for three years and I have watched you grow from boys into young men. I pray that you are good Muslim men with high moral standards. If you didn't learn anything academically, I hope you learned that who you are and what you stand for is worth more than money and the opinions of others that are not Islamically based. I'm sad to watch you go but happy you will have new experiences that will help build your characters.

There has been a shared sadness around the world but I believe you all had something special about this year. At a young age, you have had the opportunity to empathize, sympathize, and reflect. Allah says in the Quran "Verily, We shall put you to test with some fear and hunger, and with some loss of wealth, lives, and offspring. And (O Muhammad) convey good tidings to those who are patient, who say, when inflicted by hardship: Verily we are of God (his creation) and verily to Him shall we return; upon them is the blessings of Allah and His mercy" (Quran 2:155). This pandemic is our test and it has shown our strengths greatly and our weaknesses greatly. Many families have been affected in various ways and we all have been affected emotionally. Remember, this is a test and this pandemic is a testament to our characters. Reflect on who you are and make changes to enrich yourself. You all are amazing in different ways. Remember, everyone's strengths are different. Find your strength and perfect it. I hoped to give you more this school year but Allah had something greater in store for you: Reflection! Allah has allowed this virus to show us the true value of life, happiness, and people who surround you. Allah may have revealed something positive to us or negative to us, or both. Whether positive or negative, this lesson and or test will allow you to make a change. And, some of you may say, "well nothing happened," I urge you to look a little deeper to find out what lessons Allah has taught, shown, or revealed to you. I hope you all will continue to evolve into spiritually sound humans. We have had the opportunity to understand what really matters to us. Reflect!

ENTRY 104

June 29, 2020
Haala Marikar, 19 years old
Sri Lanka

I am standing in the ruins of what was once part of a castle—I
shiver,
There are little echoes of the past here,
These stone walls... what have they seen?
What would they tell me if they could speak?
Would they tell me stories of kings and queens?
Would they tell me of emperors and chieftains and nobles
and knights?
Of the battles they fought, and the victories begot?
Of betrayal and treason and scheming and lies?
Or would they tell me—these walls—
A different story
Altogether,
Neither of emperor nor crown,
But, simply, of men and women
Like you and I,
Who lived and died,
In a perpetual lust
After wealth and power,
Never once remembering
That the dust
Beneath their shoes

Was once men and women
Like me and you.

Ya Allah, help us to lead a life of sincerity and truth and simplicity and piety. Aameen.
Ya Rabb, grant us the best of both this world and the next. Aameen.

chapter Five

July 2020

COVID-19 worldwide statistics
for July 2020:[151]

New cases at the start of the month: 215557
New deaths at the start of the month: 4824

New cases at the end of the month: 278504
New deaths at the end of the month: 6336

151   Source: The New York Times

ENTRY 105

July 1, 2020
Aishah Alam, 31 years old
New York

I came across the letter below on a website called mumsad-vice.co.uk and fell in love with it. I only copied and pasted some of it but I hope it reminds me of the voice of my baby whenever she cries out to me at night.

Dear mama,

Could you wake up for a minute? I know it's hard for you to open your eyes—we haven't slept a lot yet tonight. But mama, I kinda need you right now. You see, the thing is, I feel a bit lonely at the moment. I'm laying here in my crib and I'm somewhat cold. I didn't mean to cry so I'm sorry I did. I've been trying to get your attention by making some noises for a while now but you were in such a deep sleep, you couldn't hear me. I don't know how else to get your attention. During the day, I see and hear you all make noises and I see you respond well to each other. You talk to me like that too. And I try very hard but I don't know how to do that yet. So I cry so you'll listen to me.

Mama, I'm sorry for crying. Like I said, I feel a bit

lonely. I just spent nine months inside your belly where I've always felt safe. It's a bit scary to me to be in such a big bed all by myself. I miss your heart-beat, the rushing of your blood, the warmth and the food. I miss your breathing and your hands you put over me to protect me when I still was inside your belly.

Soon, I'll be able to be there for you. Or for my brothers or sisters. Or for my friends in school. You're teaching me how to take care of someone. You're teaching me that you listen, even when I can't ask. You're teaching me I'm safe, even when sometimes it feels like I'm not. You're teaching me that you love me, even when you're very tired.

Thank you.

And mama, I love you.

Anonymous

ENTRY 106

July 1, 2020
Aishah Alam, 31 years old
New York

Is it strange that I feel like death is so near?

Sometimes I feel like I have all the days in the world but lately I haven't been feeling that way.

I feel like I've forgotten so much of myself in the haze of pregnancy and giving birth. I have forgotten where to truly pay attention and I feel like the important things keep being replaced by things which have little significance.

It is so easy to want more, to think I deserve all these gifts Allah has given me and yet I allow these same gifts to lull me to forget how fleeting everything material is, including life.

It is so easy to be distracted. So easy... and I hate it. I hate being distracted. That feeling of not doing what you are meant to do, like you keep missing the point, like you never really get it.

There are all these lights everywhere but not all of them are real. They're just false connections which ring up false emotions which distract us from what we truly feel.

We become numb. It is painful to be numb. I don't want to be numb.

And we choose to be immersed within this wipe,

swipe and like because it is painful to feel too.

I see relationships broken because we become entitled, arrogant. Thinking we deserve something when we are so focused on looking out there, when the one thing we have been looking for is right here, in here all along.

I live. I am alive. Today. And though death may come tomorrow, I pray that Allah takes me and my beloved when we are at our best, ameen.

It hurts to feel.

To love is painful. It is both painful and beautiful at the same time.

It is hard to be vulnerable because so many speak of it but something about posting emotions on social media feels...far away.

ENTRY 107

July 7, 2020
Amirah Ahmed, 16 years old
Virginia

My Truth

My truth is in the whispers of the wind on a warm summer day.

It is in the startling rumble of a car's engine at 6:30 a.m. mingling with the blaring siren of my alarm clock rousing me for the school day.

My truth is in the pinch of the safety pin securing my colorful hijab in preparation for another presentation.

It is in the flapping of the butterflies' wings in my stomach at the start line of my first cross country race.

My truth is in the pride that swells as I watch my little sister nail her routine at her gymnastics meet.

It is in the resounding defeat that sweeps the atmosphere as every crumpled sheet of poetry falls to my feet.

My truth is in the sound of the adhan on a Ramadan night as the glass of milk tantalizes my taste buds, mere feet away from the prayer rug.

My truth is in the uncertainty of the future and the undeniable concrete nature of the past.

My truth encompasses all that I am and all that I will be.

ENTRY 108

June 16, 2020
Naimah Baptiste, 32 years old
New Jersey

NO one cared until YOU...

pushed your stroller with your bags in front of the elderly couple.

No one cared until YOU hauled passed the nurse.

No one cared until YOU thought you should get on before the woman in the wheelchair

And... they all patiently waited, silently!

So, Yes there are whispers and stares!

Respect our equality and respect yourself...

Eyes widened with surprise.

She began to push her open stroller onto the NYC bus.

Eyes began to roll and attitudes began to rise.

The silent looks were given around the bus.

A secret communication that we all knew too well.

I wonder, is this secret communication only shared by us?

Does it have to do with the history that ties us together, shared by trauma?

The muffled sounds began to rise to a whisper.

The quiet whispers were everywhere...

The whispers began to rise...

Oddly it was as if we knew we had to speak out together...

Nods of agreement. "Umm hum" and "yess"

opened conversation on the bus.

"Bedstuy isn't Bedstuy anymore."

"They gentrifying the place."

"We ran y'all out before, we'll do it again."

"It's that privilege."

"Close your stroller and get on the bus."

"Don't act like you never got on the bus before."

"She don't know how to close it."

"Why she looking confused?"

"Look at her."

We all look out the window...

"I'm sure the babysitter knows how to close it."

The bus of people in their uniforms wait. Wait. And wait.

For YOU so they may go to work.

NO one cared until YOU...

pushed your stroller with your bags in front of the elderly

couple.

No one cared until YOU hauled passed the nurse.

No one cared until YOU thought you should get on before

the woman in the wheelchair

and ... they all patiently waited, silently!

So, yes there are whispers and stares!

Respect our equality and respect yourself...

And I ask you... would you have felt bad if it was a black

woman who did that?

ENTRY 109

July 12, 2020
Zainab Rahman, 17 years old
New Jersey

I have never experienced something like this
It is unreal
To see them like this
No shoes, no clothes, laying on the floor
I wish my deeds help me pass through jannah's door
Seeing those kids, tears in their eyes,
If only the world could hear their pleas, their cries
Life is a luxury
While they live in misery
To bring them happiness, a simple goal of mine,
It is a lie to say it is all fine
It is unreal to see them like this
No shoes, no clothes, laying on the floor
I wish my efforts, my deeds help improve my character,
For they may help me in the hereafter,
That is my goal, my dua,
To listen to their cries, their pleas
Don't let them die,
Do everything you can to help them survive
Jordan—an experience of a lifetime

ENTRY 110

July 21, 2020
Aishah Alam, 31 years old
New York

Life

This seed.

Planted and harvested upon the valiant womb of my mother

Fruit of her tree

My roots planted upon a resounding vigor given life in the blow of faith

fortified by a lining of mercy

As the binding of my being is strengthened only upon the seed of purity

Budding with a book whose pen has been lifted in just testimony

Paused in the breeze of my innocence

I am equipped by

All I need to become

In the bliss of my ease

I sway in the plays

Of my life

As my filament becomes imprinted in the dominion of this world

Touching but never holding the glory of this earth

Stalking the illusion of a promise for this blossom to be endless

Lockdown

Liberated bloom of a style whose relevance hangs upon
the noose of grapevines buzzing with what is current in the
temptation of magnificence
And in the peak of my youth
I ask, am I ready to fall?

Fall
I fall
 in the season of my decline
For this is the nature of life
And I fall like the night
preceded by the scorching sun of a long day
I fall like time who rebels against my control,
pledging allegiance only to my Lord
Time revealing my ardent obedience to it
submitting to ease only when I too follow its creed
I fall like the floods of my reign coming to the end of my
crusade
For every empire of every age
is destined to fall
And I fall like the conclusion of the essence of founding
souls of nations
whose posterity was wounded with luxury
I fall like the unjust ruler's sword as he sells heaven for the
pennies found in the crevices of crumbling walls
In this temporal construction of a world whose fragility I am
victim of

I fall like the fruit of heaven from the tree to the grips of my desire
Why oh
Mortal being born innocent but choosing sin
Why
obedience to the fiery whispers of the disobedient one
Oh
I see how the spirit of evil is un righteously a resilient one
For I am in the recognition of a Just Lord's promise of truth trapped in a confinement of the devil's lies
And is hell not surrounded by temptation and heaven surrounded by trials?
And in untamed Desires lay temporal satisfaction for the foolish
And this stigma upon my falling legacy
Reveals a stark reality
And I fall like two legs whose knees only know how to bend in prostration as they slap across the very soil which I was nurtured from
Planting more seeds
I can only plant my seed when I am fallen
Reaching my destination on my two knees as I crawl
Like a baby who must first be trained to bow in order to then walk
And humbled are those who believe
Giver to the bees who spread my pollen across the west and the east

Lockdown

Blown and thrown in the bitter sweet battle of my soul
Comes an end only when I am carried
Held, cradled, led
And to be led is through enlightenment
And oh how this broken bulb needs it
And to not have light is to live in darkness
And even the sharpest of eyes cannot see without His shine
And His lamp is ever burning,
In such trove
of His guidance
I am enshrouded
upon a road
To the only salvation permeable to my sinful soul
And mistake not the testimony of belief to be the bringer of ease
For God tests those whom He loves
"Or think you that you will enter Paradise without such (trials) as came to those who passed away before you? They were afflicted with severe poverty and ailments and were so shaken that even the Messenger and those who believed along with him said, 'When (will come) the Help of Allah?' Yes! Certainly, the Help of Allah is near!" (Quran 2:214).
The help of Allah is near, as I march upon the path of the messengers and prophets
And after the fall of great feats came the bringer of double the ease

Rise

Risen by Him who saved Yunus from the belly of the whale

Him, who saved Ayoub from the breaking of his skin

Him, who saved Ibrahim from the burning of the fire

Him, who saved Yusuf from the darkness of the well

Him, who saved Musa from the torrent of the Nile

Him, who saved Nuh from the flood

For hope can no longer stay fallen when knowledge of His

favors is engraved in my veins as they run with the bleeding

of the thorn of my trials,

Whose heat is present in every season

And I am shifting from season to season

beginning with an ending

Then ending with a beginning

And then beginning with no end

Immortal soul, dying a thousand deaths in every fall,

And what leaves fall will return to earth once more

And so comes the finalization of this testing abode

Am I ready to die?

Death

And now comes the season of death

"And every soul shall taste death" (Quran 3:185)

Living.

Between wakefulness and sleep

Cradled for half my life in the slumber of the unseen

And what greater detraction from the glamor

of this prison

Lockdown

Than the arrival of my departure
And my celebration is pending upon
my final deed
I am haunted by the seasoning of my prime with a taste of
beautiful things
Boxed glories familiarizing the insightful
Of boxed rooms in a cemetery
Clued in the sure tap of my feet, I send a daily siren call to
my grave,
And this is the season of the dead
Dead like the tongue void of the remembrance of its Lord,
Laying idol in submission to the whims of a stone heart
Dead like the heart of a sinner whose arrogance is solidified
in its embrace with the devil
Dead like the hope of His pleasure in the absence of the
repenter
Dead like the appetite of a believer's soul when starved of
their seclusion
Dead like the dried ink of a pen which no longer needs to
write what will be for all has been written in the book of
decrees
And what refuge can be given from certainty?
What lofty towers have ceilings which reach the skies?
Because man cannot own the stairways to heaven
Though God knows Pharaoh and Haman tried
And return like that seed do I
To a valiant womb

Delivered in the concert of such feeble cry

And at my birth came the call to prayer

And at my death is the somber funeral prayer

And unlike the seasons of this world

Water from the tears of my mourners

cannot resurrect this seed

Though the heavens and Earth cry in the departure of the righteous

And so

this soul

greets this body

once more

And from this seed grows

all I planted with it of my deeds

Whose weight can only make me content in the exclusivity of my creed

on my right lays the door to heaven

and on my left lays the door to hell

grave tribulations dictated by two faces

Who need no invitation

to attend the ceremony of the wise and the unwise

Decided by the three fundamental questions

Who is your Lord? Allah.

What was your religion? Islam.

Who was this man sent among you? Muhammed (peace be upon him)

I ask, am I ready to be revived?

Lockdown

And then comes the season of my spring
As the dead will awaken to walk upon this earth once again
And day comes out of the mourning of the loss of all that
gave life
Revived
And I will be revived
like a dead body given life in its mother's womb
Revived like the soul of a nation of believers who stand up
all night in prayer
Revived like the bonds of faith as thousands of feet join in
the unity of the praying congregation
Revived like the will of the oppressed as they amplify their
voices against the oppressors
Revived like Al Quds back in the rightful hands of the Pal-
estinians
Revived like a lion's roar as he defends his tribe
Revived like the moon whose reflection lights up every path
of the travelers on this world
Revived in the resurrection of soul and body
only to live now eternally
I am revived on the day of retribution
Standing before a Lord whose mercy is more than the moth-
er whose womb bore me
Yet His justice cannot weep, for its presence is unquestion-
able
And in this my judgement begins.
Am I ready to be surrounded by a million deaths or am I

finally living?

All my life I ask, am I ready?

FREEDOM WRITERS

THE FINAL CHAPTER

ONE YEAR LATER

ENTRY 111

April 3, 2021
R Jahan, 38 years old
New York

This Life

This life is full of lies and loss
But we have to gloss over that
And get to somewhere better anyway.

The way is hard and painful
For you and me, soulful people.
Yet we pray the awful goes away.

We have to go on our way peacefully.
We have to go on our way determinedly.
We have to reach our true destination: Jannat.

Let no liars and losers get in our way.
Let no jealous ones and haters get in our way.
Let no users and abusers block our path.

We have a mission: Destination Jannat.
You want that. I want that.
May Allah Bless us with that.

ENTRY 112

April 15, 2021
R Jahan, 38 years old
New York

Earning/Sixth Avenue

Earning a buck is hard work.
But especially in the midst of a Pandemic.

When your technology testing is overbooked
And you come back home empty-handed.

Except for the shopping trolley full of
More affordable goodies from Whole Foods!

(Sweet treats to soothe a starving-poet soul.)

ENTRY 113

April 17, 2021
R Jahan, 38 years old
New York

Musings On Death

Death is only the beginning. But what matters is, the beginning of what? Eternal paradise or eternal torment?

If you could tell the Coronavirus one thing,
what would it be?

If I could tell the Coronavirus one thing, it would be, "Moribundus sumus, non te salutamus" echoing the ancient statement of the gladiators as they entered the arena to fight the lions to the death for the Romans' entertainment. "We who are both to die do not salute you." For a grisly or unnatural death is not a celebration, it is almost an abomination, a desecration of the natural order of things.

ENTRY 114

April 17, 2021
Haala Marikar, 20 years old
Sri Lanka

When I am gone,
I don't want poetry
Written for me,
I want prayers.
Pray for me,
For my grave to welcome me
Tenderly,
For Jannah to be awaiting me.
Pray for me.
Don't write me poetry,
Don't frame my pictures,
I would rather you forgot me,
Don't dishonour my memory
By dishonouring my wishes.
Let no pictures remain
Of me.
I don't want poetry.
Only pray for me.

ENTRY 115

April 21, 2021
Haala Marikar, 20 years old
Sri Lanka

Two years on, we remember.

The explosions in the quiet of an April morning.

Church on Easter Sunday,

Breakfast at the Shangri-La,

Love and laughter and life,

Before politics and terrorists and hatred happened.

Let grief and fear and hatred

Give way to

Love, once again.

Let us heal together.

Overcome our losses,

For our pain

Is shared.

Because nobody,

Nobody was spared.

Neither those who died

Nor those left behind.

We haven't forgotten.

Two years on, we remember.

Two years on, we will still hold accountable

Those who sit on their thrones

With blood on their hands

And no guilt in their hearts.

But justice will come.

We still remember.

ENTRY 116

April 25, 2021
Nameera Fatima, 17 years old
India

The Pre and Post Pandemic Life

The year 2020 brought unseen challenges upon human kind. It's almost a year on and the virus is still upon us. The current pandemic has placed the whole world at a standstill with nations going into lockdown to stall the virus's relentless march. Still, there is no SPECIFIC data on when situations will stabilize. What is certain is that the people are learning valuable lessons through this global crisis, and life after COVID is sure to change for the better. Aristotle, the celebrated philosopher, taught, "It is during our darkest moments that we must focus to see the light." Thus, this is perhaps the right time to look ahead at expected improvements in the post-COVID world.

People learned to live with the bare essentials during the lockdown. Healthy home-cooked meals replaced junk food. Closed shopping malls highlighted the futility of mindless consumerism. As pollution levels went down and nature flourished, people realized the necessity of a sustainable lifestyle for the health of the Planet. Protection of the Earth and the next generation is going to drive a majority of life-choices.

Therefore, rather than going outdoors, people chose to relax and unwind with their family members. Thus, the lockdown brought the importance of family into focus. The post-COVID mindset brought the protection of family to the frontline as a safety net against all future contingencies.

Well, 2020 was not all about virus, vaccines, masks, maintaining physical distances. If you go back to 2020, you'd have seen there were protests which emerged in states like Michigan and Virginia as conservative activists demonstrated their opposition to the science-backed stay-at-home orders meant to slow the coronavirus's spread.

Yet an overall lack of in-person protests changed drastically following the killing of George Floyd by Minneapolis police, resulting in thousands taking to the streets. As the year continued, an increased focus on society's most systemic ills, thanks to the Black Lives Matter movement, motivated actions like Black Friday Amazon protests and U.S. election celebrations for Biden's win. Some of the protests are ongoing. We also faced so many hazards that stormed the entire planet, as there were explosions, plane crashes, storms, bush fires, forest fires and of course the contagious virus that has literally grabbed us by the throats.

And in this tight spot, we lost some of our loved ones. We also lost so many wise ulamas (scholars). Widespread deaths in general and deaths of 'ulama, one after the other in quick succession, is not a good sign. It reminds us about a Hadith that says 'ilm (i.e. knowledge) will be taken away before there is a great destruction. And deaths of 'ulama, who are carriers of the knowledge of Qur'an and Hadith, amount to knowledge and noble people being taken away. As the Hadith states: 'Abdullah Ibn 'Amr reported: The Messenger of Allah, peace and blessings be upon him, said, "Verily, Allah does not withhold knowledge by snatching it away from his servants, but rather he withholds knowledge by taking the souls of scholars, until no scholar remains and people follow ignorant leaders. They are asked and they issue judgements without knowledge. Thus, they are astray and lead others astray" (Sahih al-Bukhari 100, Sahih Muslim 2673).

May Allah (s.w.t) grant them Jannah and forgive them and those who find no one to pray for them.

The year 2020 was like a bad nightmare which can never be forgotten, nor it's lessons. Like:

- Every soul is going to taste the death, so never get too busy making your life more enjoyable that you forget your afterlife.
- Not everyone you love will always stay with you.
- No matter what circumstances come into your life, always be grateful for what you have because the secret of happiness is found in Gratitude.

- It's okay if you make no progress. The progress you've made is the lessons you've learned.
- Be proud of yourself for trying your best. As a human race, we have lost a lot this year, so celebrate the wins, even if it is only that you made it to December of 2020. THAT is worth celebrating.

This is the second Ramadan we are living with covid-19, hoping this will be the last straw In sha 'Allah. Ramadan was difficult and by hook and crook we lived through 2020. Let's pray and hope that these rules of social distancing end before the end of 2021. If Allah wills it.

ENTRY 117

April 27, 2021
Haala Marikar, 20 years old
Sri Lanka

I think about how things couldn't be more different than they were last year. Ramadan of last year was the first time my country was on lockdown because of COVID. It was a novel experience, wholesome family time, it was all that.

It was iftars with my brother and I taking turns to set the food and water on the mat for the rest of the family. It was long, hot days stuck inside my house, sitting in the sofa on the lobby among the cushions, and reciting Qur'an. It was fish patties and beef samosas straight from the Mahaiyawa bakeries some days. It was stringhoppers and pol sambol, and glasses of cool green Nannari juice. It was ordering our groceries from my best friend's family store, and yes, it was a pandemic, yes, we were afraid, but not... Not this much. We didn't have reason to be as afraid as we are now, with strains mutating at an alarming rate, and countries collapsing under the weight of no oxygen cylinders.

This year... This year, I am not even home. I am in a country I've never been to before, pursuing my undergraduate degree in my second semester. Room Number 62 of this big, old hostel—this is home away from home now. Iftar is not on the mat at home with my family, it is under the bougainvillea tree by the Chemistry Department with my best friend who is also here pursuing her own degree. I wake up for sahar to my alarm tone, but most nights, I don't sleep at all because I am swamped with assignments. The days are longer because it's summer—another novelty I've never experienced before; Sri Lanka doesn't have seasons. And the corridors echo with the sound of Urdu, and the mountains are silhouetted in the distance, much wider and bigger and rockier than the mountains back home, and the paths are stained with the juice of fallen mulberries, and all this is so new to me, and I miss my family, and this is more of an outpouring of my feelings than any structured or concrete piece of prose, but I want to say, all this is new but the novelty is what makes it exciting.

And everything will be good. Everything will be alright. Sab theek ho jayega, as they say in this new and poetic language I'm learning.

The believer's affair is always good. Trust in the decree of Allah. And remember that there is no disease that Allah has created, except that He also created its cure.

ENTRY 118

April 28, 2021
R Jahan, 38 years old
New York

You are not alone. If you feel like giving up, don't. If you feel like no one cares about you, know that your Creator does! Have hope and faith in Him. Read inspirational stories of famous prophets and how they overcame great odds to be granted success, like the story of Moses, peace be upon him, who escaped Pharaoh's oppression to freedom.

ENTRY 119

May 1, 2021
Haala Marikar, 20 years old
Sri Lanka

"Just keep breathing, mother,
Everything will be alright."

Ministers sit for interviews,
And all but roll their eyes

At the statistics and lived experiences
Of those on the frontlines.

"You will go home to your children,"
The doctor tries to smile;

When a patient is on their deathbed,
It makes no difference if you lie.

The streets are full of people
Who have lain down to die

Because the hospitals have no Oxygen left
To try and save their lives.

"Just keep breathing, mother.
Everything will be alright."

ENTRY 120

May 3, 2021
Amirah Ahmed, 16 years old
Virginia

Everything that's happened between the start of the freedom writers journals[152] and where we are today has been integral to the ultimate trajectory of our lives. While the COVID-19 pandemic may one day be a laughable tale I tell to my grandchildren, its repercussions are life-long. The loss of my senior year of high school has shaped my college process and where I will be spending my undergraduate years. The state of affairs over the past year has dramatically altered my career ambitions and will forever change my outlook on justice. The pandemic has taken people I thought would be forever, out of my life, and vice versa, and for this I am eternally grateful. In my final remarks for this phenomenal project, I tell God thank you. Thank you for the devastating losses and failures, and thank you for some of the most joyful moments of my life so far. This past year was full of purpose, and I am reaping every lesson possible from it.

---

152 This was the working name of this book.

ENTRY 121

May 5, 2021
Haala Marikar, 20 years old
Sri Lanka

For someone who's only been away from home and family for more than a few days at most, the last six months have been a little hard on me.

The homesickness creeps in at random moments, and leaves me with a lump in my throat and a wistful smile on my face. It's gotten better with time, but as Eid approaches, I feel it all the more. Through all of this, the kindness of strangers turned friends has kept me afloat, by Allah's grace. It's a bowl of kheer[153] brought from back home when my dorm-mate goes back for the holidays. It's invitations from friends to come celebrate Eid with them. It's offers to translate Urdu poetry because I said I'd love to read some. It's this "Eid Mubarak in advance" gift from my neighbour. It's all of these little kindnesses, these little sweet gestures that make us feel at home in a country that's nearly 3000 km away from home.

---

153 A chilled South Asian dessert made from slow cooked rice

ENTRY 122

May 8, 2021
Haala Marikar, 20 years old
Sri Lanka

Said Odeh, 16 years old, aspiring footballer,
was out for a stroll with his friends a few Ramadan evenings ago,
When he was killed.

Razan Najjar, 20 years old, a paramedic, was
ushering in the wounded,
When she was killed.

Faris Odeh, 14 years old, was killed with a
stone in his hand, immortalized thus in graffiti
on the streets, and in his mother's memory,
A hero, a martyr, a son, a boy, a child.

Muhammed Al Durrah, 12 years old,
was killed as he crouched behind a concrete
cylinder,
Sobbing into his father's shoulder,
As the bullets ripped through the air.

They are "incidents" on newspapers.

They are "casualties" of the "Israeli-Palestinian
conflict."

No.
They were sons and daughters with dreams of
their own,
They were boys and girls,
They were children.

They are victims of a genocide, an ethnic
cleansing.
Call it what it is. Don't colour over the truth
with your efforts at neutrality.

Because when they are stealing homes,
And putting a bullet through a child's head
because he dared to throw a stone,

When they storm into the masjid in a bid to
claim the golden dome,
When they are enacting a genocide,
You cannot be "neutral" and say "we can't
choose sides."
There is only good and evil here,
Sometimes the world IS black and white,

Lockdown

See for yourself,
Go back and read the opening lines.
There's the murderer and there's the martyred.

So who's side
Are you on?

ENTRY 123

May 11, 2021
Aishah Alam, 32 years old
New York

It has been exactly one year since the freedom writers project began.

It began in Ramadan and then the death of George Floyd happened (and a few others which didn't stay in the media for long) and Covid was rampant upon the world, the death tolls so high. So high.

Today I write to you, again in Ramadan, with George Floyd's case in the courts, and covid vaccines being released.

It is also exactly one year after I had my second baby girl. She sleeps now on her right side, the same way I slept when I carried her, her cheeks flopping over and her curly hair like a tuft of softness which layers slightly so it sits like sideburns on the side of her face.

Basically, she looks very naughty (and she is), but in an endearing way.

My older one—with her thoughtful swagger!—is now two. Back then she was still trying to keep her balance, but now, thanks to Allah, she walks confidently, and actually speaks!

I still have to blink a few times as I realize she can verbalize her thoughts. (And you would have thought that would cut the temper tantrums down, but nope! Still loud as ever... and influencing her sister to follow suit!) When she says "no want that," I look at her wide eyed and simply say, "ok, fine."

On a more serious note, today we went for an Eid shopping trip so we could prepare for it on Thursday Insha Allah—it's Tuesday today.

I also saw my grandma for the first time in a very long time, and all I can think about is how much she was smiling as she saw me and my girls. I smile now thinking about it, but then feel a little sad. There is this vulnerable humanness about so many of us. It is as if all we want is to find true peace. To be happy. Some try to get it in ways which hurt others and others try to get it by hurting themselves. And then there are those who get it by asking God to give it to them, and As Salaam, the Giver of Peace, gives it openly.

I feel like I am fighting a battle every day to be true to myself and so many times I lose myself. The only thing which keeps grounding me is my religion. It tells me what really matters, and what doesn't. It is when I practice, that I feel like my truest self. I feel this strength which nothing can seem to shake.

And then you have the things which go on outside of ourselves, the ones the peace inside is preparing us to do something about. The things which do not call for peace, but for war, and that is what I battle with in my thoughts.

How can you deal with people who shoot innocent people in masses? Who bully and try and dominate places as if it is their territory? We live in 2021, and have people carrying out a modern-day colonialist project. Why isn't anyone doing anything to stop them? Why do we fervently repeat the old lessons of history and our own bloody fights for land, over and over, even today.

What have we learnt?

A vaccine is out, and India has one of the highest death tolls in the world from this pandemic. Our holy land and third holiest place in the world as Muslims has been rampaged and bombed by Israelis (and to say this out loud seems like we have to tiptoe because you're not sure who you might offend) and all we have as social justice and advocacy are videos from the blasts. Dead bodies lined in street, mothers screaming and pounding their heads as their sons lay lifeless.

And I want to be honest. I have been trying really hard to stay away from all the things happening in the world. Just for a few moments I have wanted to use this time to think. Think for myself. And through this thinking, I have decided that our organization, The Strangers Poets,[154] will do something about all these things. Even if it is to speak out.

---

154 Now called Strange Inc.

That something is a program we will run called, Poetic Justice,[155] where we ask Muslim poets around the world to write a collaborative final poem about a cause.

I don't want to be selectively helpless anymore. I don't care if people think this is so minuscule in the grand scheme of things, because I'm not measuring it in that kind of way. I'm measuring it in the way I am able to, the part I do have control of: on that day, when I stand in front of God, and He asks me what I did, I pray I can say that I did what I could.

I needed silence during this month, so I could hear myself. Hear what matters, deep here in my purpose. And all good is from Allah.

May He ease things for all of those in pain around the world, those we know about and those we do not, Ameen.

---

155 In 2020, Strange Inc. published their first book: "Poetic Justice | An Anthology of Poems by Muslims."

ENTRY 124

May 14, 2021
R Jahan, 38 years old
New York

Antivirus Poem

Immune systems are busy.

Let's keep Corona at bay.

Let's keep Corona away!

Put on your mask.

Wear it tight and snugly.

Don't worry, it doesn't make you ugly!

Every hour or so,

Go outside and open up the mask.

Go breathe in some fresh air!

ENTRY 125

May 15, 2021
R Jahan, 38 years old
New York

Pause

I have stopped dreaming.

A toll of the Pandemic

And perpetual delays.

But I might dream again

If things seem better,

If things happen faster.

ENTRY 126

May 24, 2021
Naimah Baptiste, 33 years old
New Jersey

365 days. I have been around the Universe but I'm still standing still.
My journey began with Ramadan 2020,
slow and peaceful,
Right and meticulous,
quarantined and secured.

365 days. I have been around the Universe but I'm still standing still.
Fasting to save my soul from the fiery pits of hell
and...
I watch as others dive in headfirst
murdering men, maliced mayhem, soul-snatching, self-suffocating.

365 days. I have been around the Universe but I'm still standing still.
We thought equality was accomplished with protests of black lives mattering
but...
We watched in horror the justification of racism and brutality.

Lockdown

I can't breathe, buried into dusk, driven into a deep saturation of damp deluged darkness of corruption.

365 days. I have been around the Universe but I'm still standing still.
My Asian brothers and sisters fighting the same fight,
A fight eclipsed by equity which isn't equality.
Gunshots, gunned down, lone shooters, lude festisized bodies.
Rivalry of oppression when the goal is the same,
God is One and created us as one.

365 days. I have been around the Universe but I'm still standing still.
Divided, we are conquered and conquered are we,
Enslaved by our enlightenment, shackled and yet free,
Good as dead, dead bodies. Bodies bruised, bruised and beaten, beaten in battle for their Balad![156] Gaza.
Mothers wail while children cry, crumbling buildings bury fathers alive.
Justice! Justice! Justice!

365 days. I have been around the Universe but I'm still standing still.
Allah it began with you and it will end with you.

---

156 The Arabic word for country

My hands are raised in supplication, face wet with fear, heart pounding for peace and longing for justice
for all of the oppressed.

365 days. I have been around the Universe but I'm still standing still.
From Ramadan to Ramadan...
I wonder what next Ramadan will have us witness.

A word from Dr Hatem Al Haj

Then will you not give thought?

Allah often reminds us in the Quran to reflect. He condemns the heedlessness of those who are limited in their observation to the phenomena, while being dismissive of the noumena or realities behind them.

> *"They only know what is apparent of the worldly life"*
> *(Ar-Rūm 30:7).*

The COVID-19 pandemic caused the world many losses in many respects. However, the greatest loss would be failing to learn from its lessons.

May Allah make us among those endowed with insightful hearts.

Bios

Alma Salam
Age: 21
Sri Lanka

She is a medical undergraduate. She loves writing as a hobby because it's the most suitable way for her to express her inner thoughts. She likes to train her mind to see good in every situation. She appreciates this platform and is glad to be a freedom writer.

Amirah Ahmed
Age: 16
Fredericksberg, VA USA

She is currently a high school senior with a great interest in social justice, politics, and religion. She channels her activism through her poetry, and loves Strange Inc. for giving her voice a platform. She loves graphic and web design and hopes to pursue it as a hobby. You can find her as @amibruhh on Instagram.

Asna Khan
Age: 19
India

She is an undergraduate studying Psychology, Literature and Politics. She's a poet that incorporates individual experiences to bring life to different perspectives. It helps her connect to human emotions and truly empathize with people. She writes about oppression, racism and war.

Awesome Imam
Age: 20
Kaduna state, Nigeria-Africa

She is a poet, a spoken word artist, a Muslim and a Nigerian. She stands for inspiring awe and building "WEALTH AT HEART." She decided to rise and move forward in the past lockdown. This intention brought her great benefit in her poetry. She was able to interact with popular Nigerian and international poets. This also rekindled her talent of writing over 100 poems. You can find more of her work on Instagram and Twitter at @writes_awesome.

Aamila Sameem
Age: 24
Sri Lanka

Aamila Sameem is an English Literature graduate who lives in Sri Lanka. She's a writer and poet. She is an active voice for the Muslim community. She's a freelance writer and an ardent reader inspired through a series of novels. She plans to publish her first anthology soon. Aamila inherently believes that her writing will create a tremendous change in the world. You can find her on Instagram as @AamilaSameem and on Twitter as Aamila Sameem.

Haala Marikar
Age: 19
Sri Lanka

Haala Marikar is a 20 year old award-winning essayist, writer and poet. Her debut volume of poetry "A Thousand Paper Cranes" was published in 2019. Her writings have been published in various national and international magazines, and she has also won several awards in slam poetry. She is currently pursuing her undergraduate degree in Biotechnology at one of Pakistan's leading universities.

Maman Kabah
Age: 25
New York

She graduated with her Associates Degree in Culinary Arts, and is President of Ummahat Ul Mumineen. As part of Mother of the Believers, she strives to strengthen the bond of women through Islam.

Naimah Baptiste-Mohammed
Age: 32
New Jersey

She graduated from Medgar Evers College and is currently attending CUNY SPS. During the recording of her journals, she taught English Language Arts and American History at Al Noor School in Brooklyn. She also enjoys performing spoken word. She's a part of a research program that is exploring the effectiveness of an anti-violence and anti-anxiety program for children of all ages called B.A.S.E. (Baby Watching Against Aggression and Anxiety for Sensitivity and Empathy), overseen by a Professor in the Department of Education at CUNY Medgar Evers College.

Nameera Fatima
Age: 16
India

She has lived in the Indian countryside, famous for its customs and traditions. She's a student of Science, and a novice poet. She has a keen interest in studying Quran and modern science. You can follow her on Instagram at @nmeeera_f.

R. Jahan
Age: 38
New York

A poet by nature, she has been writing poetry since age 11. She cares about different issues and has had a challenging but interesting life. Her first book of poems, "Fever 105°: Post-9/11 Poems" is available at Amazon.com. For this project, she focused on the emotions and panic of the Pandemic.

Zainab Rahman
Age: 17
New Jersey

Holding a true passion for literary art, she has been writing for over a decade. For her, poetry is the best form of expression there is. She also conducts a poetry/spoken word club in Noor Ul Iman School (New Jersey).

Aishah Alam
Age: 32
New York

She is the founder of Strange Inc. and proudest of being a mother of two sweet girls. This project was a form of therapy for her and she hopes that her words can offer true insight into how not so strange we are as Muslims. You can find her at @aishahalam on Instagram.

Kashmir Maryam
Age: 31
Philadelphia

She is a Spoken Word Poet, Author, and mindset coach. She is also the mother of Abdurahmaan, and Khadijah. Kashmir is the co-founder of Strange Inc., and she also continues her writing and hosts regular workshops and seminars to empower young Muslim women.

About Strange Inc.

At Strange Incorporated, their paramount mission is to empower the voices of Muslim women. The organization's inception was fueled by an unwavering passion to uplift and celebrate the creative diversity within the Muslim community, particularly among its youth and their poetic talents.

Their journey began with spoken word performances, but they soon realized that their community required more. Muslim women's voices were being silenced, distorted, and misrepresented in media and politics, prompting them to take action.

For too long, biased and offensive narratives have drowned out the voices of Muslim women, and their stories have been co-opted. However, at Strange Inc., silence is no longer an option.

Guided by the Quran and the Sunnah of Muhammad (peace be upon him), they are a faith-based organization committed to truthfulness and excellence in all their endeavors.

Through collaboration, they unite Muslim creatives worldwide, mobilizing a movement for positive change through art. Their art heals and helps Muslim women reclaim their identities, rooted in faith.

Their goal is to uplift the authentic voice of Muslim women by publishing more books, teaching, and recognizing talented writers. They refuse to let the media speak for them or confine them with misconceptions about the hijab.

At Strange Inc., they fight to preserve their religious freedoms and tell their stories as women of faith, integrity, community, and culture. They take bold steps to ensure their voices resound loud and clear.

Learn more at www.strangeincorporated.org

www.ingramcontent.com/pod-product-compliance
Lightning Source LLC
Chambersburg PA
CBHW022047020426
42335CB00012B/578